KENTUCKY TRIVIA

KENTUCKY TRIVIA

COMPILED BY ERNIE & JILL COUCH

Rutledge Hill Press
NASHVILLE, TENNESSEE

Published by Rutledge Hill Press, 211 Seventh Avenue North, Nashville, Tennessee 37219

Typography by Bailey Typography, Inc.

Library of Congress Cataloging-in-Publication Data

Couch, Ernie, 1949–
    Kentucky trivia   /   compiled by Ernie and Jill Couch.
        p.   cm.
    ISBN 1-55853-095-9
    1. Kentucky — Miscellanea.   2. Questions and answers.
  I. Couch, Jill, 1948–   II. Title.
F451.5.C68   1991   91-15368
976.9′0076 — dc20   CIP

Printed in the United States of America
3 4 5 6 7 8 9 — 99 98 97 96 95

PREFACE

Today Kentucky stands as a unique blend of age-old traditions, steeped in hospitality, and the latest in high-tech advancement. Kentucky's colorful and compelling history speaks of a richly diversified land and people. Captured within these pages are some of the highlights of this rich heritage, both the known and the not so well known.

Kentucky Trivia is designed to be informative, educational, and entertaining. But most of all we hope that you will be motivated to learn more about the great state of Kentucky.

Ernie & Jill Couch

To
Darral & Charlene Dablow
and
the great people of Kentucky

TABLE OF CONTENTS

GEOGRAPHY

C H A P T E R   O N E

Q. What Kentucky town is named for the two daughters of its first settler, Robert Harrison?

A. Cynthiana (for Cynthia and Anna).

———◆———

Q. Where is the home of the General Motors Corvette Assembly Plant?

A. Bowling Green.

———◆———

Q. First called Beaver Pond, the seat of Powell County is now called by what name?

A. Stanton.

———◆———

Q. The famous hunter, soldier, and frontier scout Christopher ("Kit") Carson was born near what town in 1809?

A. Richmond.

———◆———

Q. What was the first incorporated town in Kentucky?

A. Washington.

Q. Where is Kentucky's largest rural area yard sale held?

A. Falmouth.

———◆———

Q. In what city is Kentucky Highlands Museum?

A. Ashland.

———◆———

Q. Where were Daniel Boone and his salt-making companions captured by Indians on February 7, 1776?

A. Lower Blue Licks.

———◆———

Q. Constructed in 1880, the Oldtown Covered Bridge crosses what river?

A. Little Sandy River.

———◆———

Q. Where may the unusual Vent Haven Museum of ventriloquist figures and memorabilia be seen?

A. Fort Mitchell.

———◆———

Q. Prior to 1912 what was the only town in Letcher County?

A. Whitesburg.

———◆———

Q. Why must one drive through Tennessee to reach a ten-square-mile section of extreme southwestern Kentucky?

A. A double bend of the Mississippi River separates it from the rest of the state.

Q. The Big South Fork Scenic Railway runs between Stearns and what restored mining community?

A. Blue Heron.

———◆———

Q. What is the westernmost county in the state?

A. Fulton County.

———◆———

Q. Where did Kentuckians first officially convene on December 27, 1784, to discuss the feasibility of becoming a state?

A. Danville.

———◆———

Q. Including inland water, how many square miles does Kentucky cover?

A. 40,395.

———◆———

Q. What Kentucky town is named in honor of the commander of the first ship to arrive at Jamestown, Virginia, in 1607?

A. Newport (for Christopher Newport).

———◆———

Q. In what Louisville cemetery is "fried chicken king" Colonel Harland Sanders buried?

A. Cave Hill Cemetery.

———◆———

Q. What area of Kentucky was once called the "Moonshine Capital of the World"?

A. Land Between the Lakes.

Q. Dating back to 1780, the Valley View Ferry, Kentucky's oldest continuous business, operates on the Kentucky River near what town?

A. Richmond.

Q. Near what Kentucky town does the Big Sandy River flow into the Ohio River?

A. Catlettsburg.

Q. How many counties are there in Kentucky?

A. 120.

Q. Fountain Square Park is at the heart of what city's downtown area?

A. Bowling Green.

Q. What Lawrence County town was named for the Duchess of Cumberland?

A. Louisa.

Q. Where in Graves County is the "World's Largest One-day Picnic" held?

A. Fancy Farm.

Q. When Kentucky received its statehood, what Lexington structure served temporarily as the statehouse?

A. The Sheaf of Wheat Tavern.

Q. Where is the world's largest floating fountain?

A. Louisville.

———◆———

Q. What Ohio River community is named for a nineteenth-century ironmaster from Ashland?

A. Russell (for John Russell).

———◆———

Q. Pikeville is named for what explorer of the western United States?

A. Zebulon M. Pike.

———◆———

Q. What is the third largest city in Kentucky?

A. Owensboro.

———◆———

Q. Existing from 1718 to 1754, what was the last Indian village in Kentucky?

A. Eskippakithiki.

———◆———

Q. What site was selected as the permanent location for the state capital on December 8, 1792?

A. Frankfort.

———◆———

Q. Where was central Kentucky's first post office established in 1798?

A. Danville.

Q. What Knott County community is known as the home of the world's largest gingerbread man?

A. Hindman.

———————◆———————

Q. Where does Kentucky rank in land area in comparison to the other states?

A. Thirty-seventh.

———————◆———————

Q. What is the postal abbreviation for Kentucky?

A. KY.

———————◆———————

Q. Bybee Pottery, the oldest existing pottery west of the Alleghenies, is located east of what town?

A. Richmond.

———————◆———————

Q. In 1982 what Carroll County community's downtown area was designated as a National Historic District?

A. Carrollton.

———————◆———————

Q. By what name was Greenup known prior to 1872?

A. Greenupsburg.

———————◆———————

Q. Which Kentucky county has the longest name?

A. Breckinridge.

Q. What restored isolated mountain community is situated in the Cumberland Gap Historical Park?

A. Hensley Settlement.

Q. In what region of Kentucky did slavery exist to the greatest extent?

A. The Bluegrass counties.

Q. Where is the North American International Livestock Exposition held?

A. Louisville.

Q. What Kentucky town is situated at the confluence of the Main and South Lickings rivers?

A. Falmouth.

Q. Paintsville is situated on the site of what old trading post?

A. Paint Lick Station.

Q. What Kentucky city has been called the "Barbecue Capital of the World"?

A. Owensboro.

Q. Kentucky County was created out of what county on December 6, 1776?

A. Fincastle.

Q. What is the greatest north-to-south distance in Kentucky?

A. 175 miles.

———◆———

Q. Where did Henry Clay make his first and last speeches in Kentucky?

A. Winchester.

———◆———

Q. What is the oldest settlement in the Big Sandy Valley?

A. Prestonburg.

———◆———

Q. The community of Egypt is in what county?

A. Jackson.

———◆———

Q. "Bourbon Capital of the World" is the title of what town?

A. Bardstown.

———◆———

Q. Where is the Kentucky Railway Museum?

A. Louisville.

———◆———

Q. What Garrard County town was named by its founders in 1798 for their hometown in Pennsylvania?

A. Lancaster.

Q. Where is the Patton Museum of Cavalry and Armor?

A. Fort Knox.

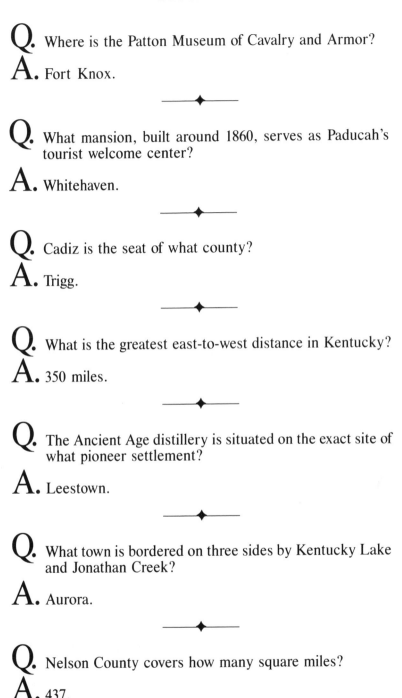

Q. What mansion, built around 1860, serves as Paducah's tourist welcome center?

A. Whitehaven.

Q. Cadiz is the seat of what county?

A. Trigg.

Q. What is the greatest east-to-west distance in Kentucky?

A. 350 miles.

Q. The Ancient Age distillery is situated on the exact site of what pioneer settlement?

A. Leestown.

Q. What town is bordered on three sides by Kentucky Lake and Jonathan Creek?

A. Aurora.

Q. Nelson County covers how many square miles?

A. 437.

Q. Where may such historic mansions as Irvinton, Bronston Palace, and Brighton be seen?

A. Richmond.

———◆———

Q. What was the site of the original Kentucky Court of Appeals?

A. Bardstown.

———◆———

Q. Where is the home of Kentucky State University?

A. Frankfort.

———◆———

Q. What is Kentucky's easternmost county?

A. Pike.

———◆———

Q. Stanford was founded in 1786 near the site of what 1775 fortification?

A. St. Asaph or Logan's Fort.

———◆———

Q. What is the oldest city in Kentucky?

A. Harrodsburg.

———◆———

Q. Built in 1828, the Maria Moore House is what city's oldest brick building?

A. Bowling Green.

Q. For whom is Somerset named?

A. The Duke of Somerset.

———◆———

Q. What town is situated at the confluence of the Cumberland and South Fork rivers?

A. Burnside.

———◆———

Q. Where may an authentic reproduction of Kentucky's first courthouse square be seen?

A. Danville.

———◆———

Q. What was the seat of Creary County prior to 1913?

A. Pine Knot.

———◆———

Q. Built in 1905–06 and noted for its neoclassical style, the Adath Israel Temple is in what city?

A. Louisville.

———◆———

Q. What Grant County town was first called Campbell's Station?

A. Dry Ridge.

———◆———

Q. Where is Eastern Kentucky University situated?

A. Richmond.

Q. What town grew up around the state's first tollgate?

A. Pineville.

Q. The Merritt Jones Tavern, which served as both a Confederate hospital and a Union commissary during the Civil War, is near what community?

A. Big Hill.

Q. For what naval hero of the War of 1812 was Hazard named?

A. Oliver Hazard Perry.

Q. What Bardstown facility houses the Oscar Getz Museum of Whiskey History?

A. Spalding Hall.

Q. The Indians called the Cumberland Gap by what name?

A. Quasioto (pronounced Wah-see-o-to).

Q. What Bell County town was named for an iron-producing center in the English Midlands?

A. Middlesboro.

Q. Featuring the only complete public collection of Jim Beam decanters, Jim Beam's American Outpost Museum may be visited in what city?

A. Louisville.

Q. Where is the forest supervisor's office of the Daniel Boone National Forest?

A. Winchester.

———◆———

Q. What two communities with names consisting of only three letters are in Clinton County?

A. Bug and Ida.

———◆———

Q. Burnside, which was renamed in honor of a Union general, was originally known by what name?

A. Point Isabel.

———◆———

Q. What town is the home of Union College?

A. Barbourville.

———◆———

Q. What Paducah house was the home of U.S. vice president Alben William Barkley from 1937 to 1956?

A. The Angles.

———◆———

Q. Where is the State Vocational and Technical School?

A. Madisonville.

———◆———

Q. The Indian battle of Shiloh was fought in defense of what sacred place?

A. Little Eagle Falls.

Q. What community for senior citizens is situated on Jonathan Creek near Aurora?

A. Lakeland Wesley Village.

Q. Where is the Kentucky Derby Museum?

A. Louisville (Churchill Downs).

Q. What community uses a log cabin built in 1867 for its Visitor Information Center and Pioneer Museum?

A. Cadiz.

Q. Boyle County was created in 1842 from portions of what two counties?

A. Mercer and Lincoln.

Q. For whom was Fort Mitchell named in 1862?

A. Prof. Ormsby Mitchell.

Q. Featuring the world's largest collection of Coca-Cola memorabilia, Schmidt's Coca-Cola Museum is to be found in what city?

A. Elizabethtown.

Q. What Russell County town was first named Jacksonville in honor of Andrew Jackson?

A. Jamestown.

Q. For what Chickasaw leader was Paducah named?

A. Chief Paduke.

———◆———

Q. Where may Morgan Row, the state's oldest row houses, be seen?

A. Harrodsburg.

———◆———

Q. New Haven was first known by what name?

A. Pottinger's Landing.

———◆———

Q. Where is the Old Mud Meeting House which housed the first Dutch Reformed Church west of the Alleghenies?

A. Harrodsburg.

———◆———

Q. What town is situated just below the confluence of the Nolin River's three branches?

A. Hodgenville.

———◆———

Q. Hustonville was originally given what name?

A. New Store (later Huston's Villa).

———◆———

Q. From 1900 to 1906 where were the persons charged with conspiracy to murder Gov. William Goebel tried?

A. Georgetown (Scott County Courthouse).

Q. Russell Springs was known to early settlers by what name?

A. Big Boiling Springs.

Q. Where is the famous clairvoyant Edgar Cayce buried?

A. Hopkinsville.

Q. In what town did the Confederate Sovereignty Convention meet and vote for Kentucky to secede from the Union?

A. Russellville.

Q. What was the original name of Mount Washington?

A. Mount Vernon.

Q. Where is the "World's Smallest House of Worship"?

A. Crestview Hills (Thomas More College).

Q. What Kentucky city is second only to New York City in its number of nineteenth-century stone and cast iron buildings?

A. Louisville.

Q. Rebecca–Ruth bourbon candy is manufactured in what city?

A. Frankfort.

Q. In 1917 what town, along with 33,000 acres, was purchased by the U.S. government on which to establish Camp Knox (Fort Knox)?

A. Stithton.

Q. Which county is named in honor of a soldier who died at the battle of the River Raisin?

A. Allen (for Col. John Allen).

Q. What Hardin County town was laid out in a wheel pattern?

A. Elizabethtown.

Q. The postmaster at Louisa named what Martin County town after his daughter?

A. Inez (for Inez Frank).

Q. In 1860 what Magoffin County town changed its name from Adamsville?

A. Salyersville.

Q. Situated midway between Paris and Mount Sterling, North Middletown was originally known by what name?

A. Swinneytown (later Middletown).

Q. What Allen County town is named in honor of Kentucky's fourth governor?

A. Scottsville (for Gen. Charles Scott).

Q. In 1780 Robert and George Moore founded what city?

A. Bowling Green.

---◆---

Q. What is the nickname for the famed 101st Airborne Division stationed at Fort Campbell, which straddles the Kentucky-Tennessee line?

A. The Screaming Eagles.

---◆---

Q. John Young Brown, who served as governor of Kentucky from 1891 to 1895, was a native of what town?

A. Elizabethtown.

---◆---

Q. The old post road, which became U.S. 41, was known to the pioneers by what name?

A. Buttermilk Road.

---◆---

Q. What was the colloquial meaning of the term *horse* from which came the names of Horse Cave and the town that grew up around it?

A. "Large."

Q. What Webster County community was named in honor of Kentucky's lieutenant governor from 1844 to 1848?

A. Dixon (for Archibald Dixon).

---◆---

Q. According to local legend, what Graves County creek and town are named in memory of a murdered Mississippi gambler?

A. Mayfield.

Q. In 1867 what state-line community was named for a president of the Louisville and Nashville Railroad?

A. Guthrie (for James Guthrie).

———◆———

Q. What Hopkins County community boasted having fifty hotels and boarding houses in the early 1900s?

A. Dawson Springs.

———◆———

Q. Mills Point is the former name of what Mississippi River town?

A. Hickman.

———◆———

Q. What Kentucky county was formed in 1784 and named for a former Virginia governor?

A. Nelson (for Thomas Nelson).

———◆———

Q. A drilled or bored well was the source of what Carlisle County placename?

A. Bardwell.

———◆———

Q. Where is the Pennyroyal Area Museum?

A. Hopkinsville.

———◆———

Q. In what city was the Episcopal Theological Seminary established in 1834 in the home of Thomas January?

A. Lexington.

Q. What was the first seat of Hickman County?

A. Columbus.

———◆———

Q. The Colville Covered Bridge, built in 1877 across Hinkston Creek, is near what Bourbon County community?

A. Millersburg.

———◆———

Q. Where did the Kavanaugh Academy open in 1903?

A. Lawrenceburg.

———◆———

Q. From what Fulton County community did John Luther ("Casey") Jones derive his nickname?

A. Cayce.

———◆———

Q. What Bardstown house has been the home of two Kentucky governors and one Louisiana governor?

A. Wickland.

———◆———

Q. Greensburg is built on the site of what 1777 settlement?

A. Glover's Station.

———◆———

Q. The seat of Clay County is named for what great English cotton processing and manufacturing center?

A. Manchester.

Q. In 1826 what Hickman County town was platted by James Gibson?

A. Clinton.

———◆———

Q. Where did Confederate forces stretch a massive chain across the Mississippi River to prevent Union gunboats from coming down the river?

A. Iron Banks (at Columbus).

———◆———

Q. The unique Woolridge monuments of Maplewood Cemetery may be seen at what town?

A. Mayfield.

———◆———

Q. Near what city did Gen. George Rogers Clark die on February 4, 1818?

A. Louisville.

———◆———

Q. In what county is Octagon Hall, the unusual eight-sided brick house built in the 1850s by Andrew Jackson Caldwell?

A. Simpson.

———◆———

Q. In 1865 what town became the seat of Lewis County?

A. Vanceburg.

———◆———

Q. The Kentucky Historical Society was founded in what city in 1836?

A. Frankfort.

Q. What are Kentucky's two best known "Shakertowns"?

A. Pleasant Hill and South Union.

Q. Featuring a genealogical library and historical museum, the national headquarters of the Sons of the American Revolution is in what city?

A. Louisville.

Q. What state highway was called the Mary Ingles Trail?

A. Kentucky 10.

Q. Germantown was known by what name when laid out by Whitfield Craig in 1784?

A. Buchanan Station.

Q. Which county's courthouse is based on a design originally proposed for the state capitol?

A. Bourbon.

Q. Woodward's Crossing evolved into what Bracken County town?

A. Brooksville.

Q. The Daniel Trabue House, built around 1823, is in which Adair County community?

A. Columbia.

Q. What was the original name of Bardstown?

A. Salem.

———◆———

Q. In 1861 what city was declared the Confederate capital of Kentucky?

A. Bowling Green.

———◆———

Q. Why is the area of Kentucky stretching along the southern border from the Appalachian Plateau to Kentucky Lake called the Pennyroyal Region?

A. It is named for a small herb of the mint family that is common in the region.

———◆———

Q. Thirteen families from the Rappahannock River region of Virginia founded what Carroll County community in 1809?

A. Ghent.

———◆———

Q. Which Kentucky county is named in honor of a casualty of the battle of Tippecanoe?

A. Owen County (for Col. Abraham Owen).

———◆———

Q. Constructed in 1854 of rough-hewn sandstone, the Cottage Iron Furnace is in what county?

A. Estell.

———◆———

Q. Where is the Gratz Park Historic District?

A. Lexington.

Q. Bison herds trampling down the soil around a mineral spring led to the naming of what Scott County community?

A. Stamping Ground.

———◆———

Q. In what town does the Yatesville Covered Bridge cross Blaine Creek?

A. Lawrence.

———◆———

Q. Where was Jefferson Davis, president of the Confederate States of America, born on June 3, 1808?

A. Fairview.

———◆———

Q. What is the third oldest incorporated town in the state?

A. New Castle.

———◆———

Q. Where is the only replica in the United States of the traditional tomb of Jesus?

A. Covington (Garden of Hope).

———◆———

Q. A U.S. senator from Missouri is honored in the name of what Marshall County town?

A. Benton (for Thomas Hart Benton).

———◆———

Q. Where in Scott County was a Choctaw Indian school established by Col. Richard M. Johnson in 1825?

A. Blue Spring.

Q. What is the former name of the community of Pewee Valley?

A. Smith's Station.

———◆———

Q. Where is the Kentucky Military History Museum?

A. Frankfort.

———◆———

Q. A large number of mineral springs ideal for a spa led to the name of what county?

A. Bath County.

———◆———

Q. Where may the childhood home of Mary Todd Lincoln be visited?

A. Lexington.

———◆———

Q. What was the meaning of the name *Chattaroy* that the Indians gave to the Big Sandy River?

A. "River of sand bars."

———◆———

Q. Alex Curran laid out what town around 1800 at the mouth of Beaver Creek on Licking River?

A. Claysville.

———◆———

Q. What town is named in honor of General Lafayette's French estate?

A. La Grange.

Q. In 1799 Dr. John Beniss founded what Nelson County town on Simpson Creek?

A. Bloomfield.

———◆———

Q. What new name was given to Hobb's Station when it was incorporated as a town in 1876?

A. Anchorage.

———◆———

Q. Eddies in the Cumberland River brought about the name of what Lyon County town?

A. Eddyville.

———◆———

Q. Holly Rood, the 1813 mansion of Gov. James A. Clark, may be seen in what town?

A. Winchester.

———◆———

Q. What was the meaning of the name *Oki-se-jib-kith-ke* which the Shawnee applied to the Big Sandy valley?

A. "Where buffalo are plenty."

———◆———

Q. Between what two towns did Kentucky's first stage-coach line run?

A. Lexington and Olympian Springs (then called Mud Lick).

———◆———

Q. Fort Vienna, which was founded in 1788, evolved into what McLean County town?

A. Calhoun.

Q. What Clark County town was named by its founder, John Baker, for his Virginia hometown?

A. Winchester.

———◆———

Q. Prior to 1879, by what name was Central City known?

A. Morehead's Horse Mill.

———◆———

Q. Kosmos Portland Cement Company established what company town in Kentucky?

A. Kosmosdale.

———◆———

Q. Although pastures seeded with Kentucky bluegrass actually have a bluish tint during the late-May blooming season, why do visitors rarely see the blue color?

A. Most of the fields are mowed or cropped by livestock.

———◆———

Q. What is the seat of Hancock County?

A. Hawesville.

———◆———

Q. Recognized as one of the state's finest examples of Greek revival architecture, the McClure-Barbee House is in what city?

A. Danville.

———◆———

Q. By what two previous names was Maceo known?

A. Rosebud and Power's Station.

Q. Though it was first called Lyon Inn, from what second name did the present name of the town of Hartford evolve?

A. Deer Crossing (a "hart ford").

———◆———

Q. In what county is Joy?

A. Livingston.

———◆———

Q. Under what name was Maysville established by the Virginia legislature in 1787?

A. Limestone.

———◆———

Q. What town grew out of the old stockaded village of Red Banks?

A. Henderson.

———◆———

Q. Dating back to 1797, the Mordecai Lincoln House is near what Washington County town?

A. Springfield.

———◆———

Q. Where did Dr. L. L. Pinkerton found the Kentucky Female Orphan Home in 1849?

A. Midway.

———◆———

Q. Prior to 1848, what was the seat of Mason County?

A. Washington.

Q. From what promontory did Daniel Boone and John Finley get their first view of the Bluegrass Uplands?

A. Pilot Knot.

———◆———

Q. Dating back to the 1780s, the Duncan Tavern is in what city?

A. Paris.

———◆———

Q. Yellow Brick and Rossborough were early names of what city?

A. Owensboro.

———◆———

Q. The last territorial governor of Nebraska, the second territorial governor of Minnesota, and a Missouri and an Ohio governor were all born in what county?

A. Fleming.

———◆———

Q. What community served as the seat of Livingston County from 1798 to 1842?

A. Salem.

———◆———

Q. Where was the first post office and distribution point for Kentucky and Northwest Territory mail?

A. Washington.

———◆———

Q. The Cumberland River was known to the Indians by what name?

A. *Shawanese.*

Q. What Bourbon County town was first called Hopewell when it was established in 1789?

A. Paris.

————◆————

Q. Smith Town at the mouth of the Cumberland River grew into what present-day town?

A. Smithland.

————◆————

Q. Constructed in 1857, Jacobs Hall at the Kentucky School for the Deaf is in what city?

A. Danville.

————◆————

Q. What town is the home of the Maker's Mark Distillery?

A. Loretto.

————◆————

Q. Dating from 1855 Bennets Mill Covered Bridge spans what stream?

A. Tygarts Creek.

————◆————

Q. Where is the Mountain Life Museum?

A. Levi Jackson Wilderness Road State Park.

————◆————

Q. Where is the Basilica of the Assumption, known as the "American Notre Dame"?

A. Covington.

ENTERTAINMENT

Q. What was the first number one single for the Judds?

A. "Mama, He's Crazy."

———◆———

Q. Louisville-born Tod Browning directed what 1931 horror classic?

A. *Dracula.*

———◆———

Q. What community is host to the Mountain Folk Dance Festival?

A. Berea.

———◆———

Q. Diane Sawyer joined what Louisville television station as a reporter in 1966?

A. WLKY–TV.

———◆———

Q. What Kentucky native appeared in the films *Major Dundee, The Wild Bunch, Dillinger,* and *The Border?*

A. Warren Oates.

Q. Tom T. Hall penned what million-seller for Jeannie C. Riley in 1968?

A. "Harper Valley PTA."

Q. In what county was country/western performer Bob Atcher born on May 11, 1914?

A. Hardin County.

Q. Where is the Poke Sallet Festival & Homecoming held?

A. Harlan.

Q. What country/rock group from Metcalfe and Barren counties walked away with three Country Music Association awards in 1990?

A. The Kentucky HeadHunters.

Q. Country music performers Bill and Cliff Carlisle were born in what community?

A. Wakefield.

Q. What vice president of the United States was the great-grandfather of Kentucky-born black jazz sensation Edith Wilson?

A. John Cabell Breckinridge (1857–61).

Q. Banjo picker J. D. Crowe is a native of what Kentucky city?

A. Lexington.

Q. What Kentuckian directed such thrillers as *Halloween,
The Fog, Escape from New York,* and *The Thing*?

A. John Carpenter.

———◆———

Q. Where did singer/actress Florence Henderson attend
school in Owensboro?

A. St. Francis Academy.

———◆———

Q. The McLain Family Band, noted for their authentic Appalachian music, were originally from what community?

A. Hindman.

———◆———

Q. What unique festival is held each spring at Washington?

A. Chocolate Festival.

———◆———

Q. In what year did the Judds receive their first Vocal Group
of the Year award from the Country Music Association?

A. 1985.

———◆———

Q. Where was jazz singer Edith Wilson born on September
2, 1906?

A. Louisville.

———◆———

Q. Comic character actor Billy Gilbert was born in what
city in 1894?

A. Louisville.

Q. What is the actual name of country picker/singer Grandpa Jones?

A. Louis Marshall Jones.

———◆———

Q. What Greenwich Village solo jazz pianist of the 1950s and early 1960s was born in Bowling Green on October 26, 1896?

A. Henry ("Hank") Duncan.

———◆———

Q. Which state park is host to the Great American Dulcimer Convention?

A. Pine Mountain State Resort Park.

———◆———

Q. Actor Leo Burmester attended what Kentucky college?

A. Western Kentucky University.

———◆———

Q. In what year was the movie *The Kentuckian* released?

A. 1955.

———◆———

Q. R. Dale Butts, who created scores for such television western series as "Laramie," "Wagon Train," and "The Virginian," was born in what community?

A. Lamasco.

———◆———

Q. Veteran member of Bob Crosby's band Julian Clifton ("Matty") Matlock was born in what Kentucky city in 1909?

A. Paducah.

Q. Billed as the "Original Authentic Folksinger," what Kentuckian was the first performer to introduce mountain music to radio?

A. Bradley Kincaid.

———◆———

Q. What 1978 single for John Conlee charted in the Top 5 country releases?

A. "Rose-colored Glasses."

———◆———

Q. In 1973 what Kentucky-born duo became the first bluegrass/country act to perform at Harrah's Club at Lake Tahoe?

A. The Osborne Brothers.

———◆———

Q. What Florence-born country instrumentalist and singer was known as the "Round Mound of Sound"?

A. Kenny Price.

———◆———

Q. In what 1918 film did Kentucky actor Henry Hull make his screen debut?

A. *The Volunteer.*

———◆———

Q. What town is host to the Washington County Sorghum Festival?

A. Springfield.

———◆———

Q. Who was the leading lady in D. W. Griffith's 1930 movie, *Abraham Lincoln*?

A. Una Merkel.

Q. On what television series did Red Foley co-star with Fess Parker?

A. "Mr. Smith Goes to Washington."

———◆———

Q. What was the name of Tom T. Hall's first country band?

A. Kentucky Travellers.

———◆———

Q. Originally scribbled on the back of a blank check, what song became a giant hit for Martha Carson in 1951?

A. "Satisfied."

———◆———

Q. Victor Mature, who was born in Louisville in 1916, made his screen debut in what 1939 film?

A. *The Housekeeper's Daughter.*

———◆———

Q. What native of Pinch-em-tight Holler organized the Renfro Valley Barn Dance's popular Coon Creek Girls?

A. Lily Mae Ledford.

———◆———

Q. Esteemed stage and screen performer Tom Powers was born in what town on July 7, 1890?

A. Owensboro.

———◆———

Q. What was the real name of character actor Rags Ragland who was born in Louisville in 1905?

A. John Morgan Ragland.

Q. What Bourbon County-born trumpeter/singer was featured at the 1969 London Jazz Expo?

A. William ("Bill") Johnson Coleman.

———◆———

Q. Crystal Gayle's name was inspired by what fast-food chain?

A. Krystal Hamburgers.

———◆———

Q. What Kentucky town renamed a three-mile section of U.S. 62 as Everly Brothers Boulevard?

A. Central City.

———◆———

Q. Livingston is the birthplace of what country music pioneer and founder of the Cumberland Ridge Runners?

A. John Lair.

———◆———

Q. What early star of country radio was born in Creek in 1911?

A. Lazy Jim Day.

———◆———

Q. With what Corbin native did Skeeter Davis team up in high school to form the successful vocal duo the Davis Sisters?

A. Betty Jack Davis.

———◆———

Q. What stage and screen actor was born Yewell Tompkins in Owensboro in 1909?

A. Tom Ewell.

Q. What fall event held in Point Park at Carrollton is known for its top musical entertainment, rodeo, and carnival rides?

A. Carroll County Tobacco Festival.

Q. In 1937 Benjamin Francis ("Whitey") Ford, John Lair, Red Foley, and Cotton Foley started what long-running country music show?

A. Renfro Valley Barn Dance.

Q. What country music superstar was born in Butcher's Hollow on April 14, 1935?

A. Loretta Lynn.

Q. Where was the Kentucky HeadHunters' "Dumas Walker" music video shot in December 1989?

A. Tompkinsville.

Q. What second-time-around release became a Top 10 hit for Gary Stewart in 1974?

A. "Drinkin' Thing."

Q. Several popular bands perform on the courthouse square during what summer musical event at Franklin?

A. Misty Mountain Concert.

Q. What was Stringbean's real name?
A. David Akeman.

Q. What was the name of the first label to record Kentucky-born blues great Helen Humes in 1927?

A. Okeh.

———————◆———————

Q. More than 50,000 people attend what annual spring celebration at Pikeville?

A. Hillbilly Days.

———————◆———————

Q. What was the actual name of Red Foley?

A. Clyde Julian Foley.

———————◆———————

Q. Country singer John Conlee was born in what town on August 11, 1946?

A. Versailles.

———————◆———————

Q. What epic motion picture was directed by D. W. Griffith in 1915?

A. *Birth of a Nation.*

———————◆———————

Q. In 1957 what became the first smash hit for the Everly Brothers?

A. "Bye Bye Love."

———————◆———————

Q. What Louisville-born blues singer recorded with her own group, the Brown Skin Syncopators, in 1922?

A. Sara ("Sarah") Martin.

Q. Where is the Fiddlers and Bluegrass Jamboree held?

A. Scottsville.

———————◆———————

Q. Jazz singer Kerry Price is a native of what Kentucky city?

A. Louisville.

———————◆———————

Q. For six years Red Foley produced and starred on what ABC television show?

A. "Ozark Mountain Jubilee."

———————◆———————

Q. Old-time southern harmony singing featuring "shape note" music is a part of what annual event at Benton?

A. The Big Singing.

———————◆———————

Q. What was the title of the Judds' first single for RCA that in 1983 broke into country music's Top 20?

A. "Had a Dream."

———————◆———————

Q. At what Morehead radio station did Tom T. Hall work as a DJ?

A. WMOR.

———————◆———————

Q. What country music pioneer and long-time member of the WLS National Barn Dance was born in Harlan County on January 26, 1899?

A. "Doc" Howard Hopkins.

Q. What country music singer was born Brenda Gail Webb in Paintsville in 1951?

A. Crystal Gayle.

———◆———

Q. "Heartaches by the Number," "I've Got a Tiger by the Tail," and "I Fall to Pieces" are just a few of the great country hits composed by what native Kentuckian?

A. Harlan Howard.

———◆———

Q. What town is host to the Black Patch Tobacco Festival that was started in 1937?

A. Princeton.

———◆———

Q. Who played Dagwood in twenty-eight "Blondie" films?

A. Arthur Lake.

———◆———

Q. Where was actress Patricia Neal born in 1926?

A. Packard.

———◆———

Q. Banjo and guitar picker Carl Jackson, who worked with Glenn Campbell for twelve years, was born in what Kentucky city in 1953?

A. Louisville.

———◆———

Q. Country music and mountain-style square dancing are featured at what celebration held each May at Pine Mountain State Resort Park?

A. Shindig in the Mountains.

Q. What was the actual name of early protest singer Aunt Mollie Jackson?

A. Mary Magdalene Garland.

———◆———

Q. What Kentucky singer/actress appeared in such movies as *Here Come the Girls, Red Garters, White Christmas,* and *Deep in My Heart*?

A. Rosemary Clooney.

———◆———

Q. Jamestown is the site of what October celebration?

A. Pumpkin Festival.

———◆———

Q. Television game show host Chuck Woolery was born in what Kentucky city?

A. Ashland.

———◆———

Q. Louisville-born actress Sean Young appeared in what 1982 high adventure science fiction movie?

A. *Bladerunner*.

———◆———

Q. What southern gospel group is based in Waco?

A. The Bishops.

———◆———

Q. In 1962 what release earned Skeeter Davis her first gold record?

A. "The End of the World."

Q. Where was actress Irene Dunne born in 1904?

A. Louisville.

———◆———

Q. Featuring bluegrass music, square dancing, a parade, and a flea market, the annual Apple Blossom Festival is held in what community?

A. Elkhorn.

———◆———

Q. In what year was Grandpa Jones inducted into the Country Music Hall of Fame?

A. 1978.

———◆———

Q. What Mayfield-born trumpeter was for several years a member of the Radio City Music Hall orchestra?

A. Richard ("Dick") Thomas Vance.

———◆———

Q. Where was actor William Conrad born on September 27, 1920?

A. Louisville.

———◆———

Q. Country and bluegrass bands, a tobacco cutting and spitting contest, and a parade are just a few of the events at what fall celebration at Sandy Hooks?

A. Elliott County Tobacco Festival.

———◆———

Q. What community was the birthplace of multitalented Merle Travis?

A. Rosewood.

Q. Henry Warren, who was born in Taylor County in 1903, was the leader and MC of what old-time string band?

A. Uncle Henry's Original Kentucky Mountaineers.

Q. Pioneer folksinger Bradley Kincaid was born in what community on July 13, 1894?

A. Point Leavall.

Q. Such entertainment as a bed race, fireworks, horse show, and graffiti contest are all a part of what Mayfield spring celebration?

A. Mayfest.

Q. In 1990 what city honored the Judds by renaming its 16th Street Plaza, "Judd Plaza"?

A. Ashland.

Q. What bluegrass music event which draws several thousand fans is held each June at Kentucky Horse Park?

A. Festival of the Bluegrass.

Q. Don Everly of the Everly Brothers was born in what community on February 1, 1937?

A. Brownie.

Q. What actress played the role of Loretta Lynn in the movie *Coal Miner's Daughter*?

A. Sissy Spacek.

Q. What was the name of Charlie Monroe's long-time band?

A. The Kentucky Pardners.

———◆———

Q. Elizabethtown is the site of what summer celebration?

A. Kentucky Heartland Festival.

———◆———

Q. Where was Bill Monroe, "the man who invented blue-grass music," born on September 13, 1911?

A. Rosine.

———◆———

Q. In addition to such stage names as Mountain Fern and Dixie Lee, by what name was the 1940s country singer LeVerne Williamson best known?

A. Molly O'Day.

———◆———

Q. Where is the Cloggers Festival held?

A. Renfro Valley Country Music Center.

———◆———

Q. What Kentucky native appeared in such films as *Adam's Rib, Up Front, State Fair,* and *The Great Gatsby*?

A. Tom Ewell.

———◆———

Q. The award-winning gospel group of the 1960s and 1970s, the Happy Goodman Family, was headquartered for many years in what Kentucky community?

A. Madisonville.

Q. What Brooksville-born screen actor appeared in *Gunfight in Abilene, The Ride to Hangman's Tree,* and *Rough Night in Jericho?*

A. Don Galloway.

Q. Progressive bluegrass pickers Bob and Sonny, the Osborne Brothers, were both born in what Kentucky community?

A. Hyden.

Q. What was Boots Randolph's 1963 smash hit?
A. "Yakety Sax."

Q. Julian Goodman, who became chairman of the board at NBC in 1974, was born in what town?

A. Glasgow.

Q. What Cordell native has received both Male Vocalist of the Year and Entertainer of the Year awards from the Country Music Association?

A. Ricky Skaggs.

Q. Crystal Gayle is a sister to what country music star?
A. Loretta Lynn.

Q. Jazz pianist Herman Chittison, who became a favorite in New York's East Side supper clubs during the 1940s and 1950s, was born in what Kentucky town?

A. Flemingsburg.

Q. Where was Country Music Hall of Fame member Red Foley born on June 17, 1910?

A. Blue Lick.

———◆———

Q. What Kentucky-born actor played the role of Jefferson Davis in the 1940 movie *Virginia City*?

A. Charles Middleton.

———◆———

Q. In the 1944 box-office hit *Double Indemnity*, what Kentucky native played Barbara Stanwyck's husband and victim?

A. Tom Powers.

———◆———

Q. What gospel music event, begun in 1950, is held each Labor Day weekend at Breaks Interstate Park?

A. Autumn Gospel Song Festival.

———◆———

Q. Kentucky native Kenny Price had his first Top 10 country hit with what 1966 recording?

A. "Walking on New Grass.

———◆———

Q. Saxophonist Homer Louis ("Boots") Randolph III is a native of what Kentucky city?

A. Paducah.

———◆———

Q. What was the title of Ricky Skaggs's first album to be acclaimed?

A. "Sweet Temptation."

Q. The Kentucky Wool Festival, featuring such events as bluegrass music, heritage demonstrations, and a muzzleloader competition, is held at what town?

A. Falmouth.

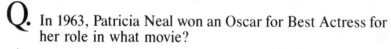

Q. In 1963, Patricia Neal won an Oscar for Best Actress for her role in what movie?

A. *Hud.*

Q. What first album for the Kentucky HeadHunters on Mercury/Polygram went platinum?

A. *Pickin' on Nashville.*

Q. Honky-tonk singer/songwriter Gary Stewart was born in what county in 1945?

A. Letcher County.

Q. What was Martha Carson's maiden name?

A. Amburgey.

Q. What musical competition is held on the courthouse lawn at Harrodsburg each August?

A. Old Time Fiddlers' Contest.

Q. What dance team provides entertainment at the University of Louisville's football and basketball games?

A. The Ladybirds.

Q. What Henderson-born blues performer was known for such songs as "Bootleggin' Ain't Good No More," "Built Right on the Ground," and "Lawdy, Lawdy Worried Blues"?

A. Theodore ("Blind Blues") Darby.

———◆———

Q. What vaudeville and blues performer was born Rosa Deschamps at Henderson on November 24, 1896?

A. Rosa ("Rose") Henderson.

———◆———

Q. In the 1940s Kentuckian Bob Atcher was the mainstay of what Chicago country music radio program?

A. WLS National Barn Dance.

———◆———

Q. Banjo picker Stringbean was known by what additional stage title?

A. "The Kentucky Wonder."

———◆———

Q. What Kentuckian composed and recorded the country hit "Old Dogs, Children, and Watermelon Wine"?

A. Tom T. Hall.

———◆———

Q. With an annual attendance of over 500,000, where is the Kentucky State Fair held?

A. Louisville.

———◆———

Q. Edith Wilson appeared in a nonsinging role in what 1940 movie?

A. *I'm Still Alive.*

Q. What important early movie innovator and director was born in La Grange in 1875?

A. D. W. Griffith.

———◆———

Q. Country music songwriter and performer Harlan Howard was born in what Kentucky city in 1929?

A. Lexington.

———◆———

Q. What jazz musician and composer was born in Wayland on September 25, 1937?

A. Horacee Arnold.

———◆———

Q. Live entertainment, a reunion dinner, and pageants make up part of the activities of what August celebration at Salyersville?

A. Magoffin County Founders Day Festival.

———◆———

Q. In what movie did Merle Travis play a guitar-strumming sailor?

A. *From Here to Eternity.*

———◆———

Q. In what year did John Conlee join the Grand Ole Opry?

A. 1979.

———◆———

Q. Known best for his jazz clarinet, Kentuckian "Matty" Matlock recorded what LP album on the Warner Brothers label?

A. *Paducah Patrol.*

Q. What Lexington-born jazz performer/composer was responsible for discovering and presenting Roberta Flack?

A. Leslie Coleman ("Les") McCann.

Q. Where is the Pendleton County Homecoming held?

A. Falmouth.

Q. What country/gospel performer was born in Neon on March 19, 1921?

A. Martha Carson.

Q. What Kentucky native enjoyed success in his singing career during the late 1960s and early 1970s with such songs as "With These Hands" and "Compared to What"?

A. Les McCann.

Q. In what 1982 Clint Eastwood movie did Merle Travis make his last film appearance?

A. *Honky Tonk Man*.

Q. What premier jazz guitarist of the 1940s and 1950s was born in Louisville on August 20, 1927?

A. James ("Jimmy") Elbert Raney.

Q. What ailment curtailed the soaring country music career of Pike County native Molly O'Day in 1952?

A. Tuberculosis.

Q. The score for the 1970s movie *No Place to Hide* was written by what Livingston County native?

A. Michael Joseph Smith.

———◆———

Q. Country artist Billy Edd Wheeler received a BA degree from what Kentucky college?

A. Berea College.

———◆———

Q. In 1991 what country/rock group created a music video based on the theme song of Walt Disney's popular "Davy Crockett" series of the mid-1950s?

A. The Kentucky HeadHunters.

———◆———

Q. What Kentucky actress had to deal with W. C. Fields as her daddy in the 1940 movie *Bank Dick*?

A. Una Merkel.

———◆———

Q. Country singer Dwight Yoakam is a native of what town?

A. Pikeville.

———◆———

Q. What blues guitarist was born in Morganfield in 1911?

A. John Tyler ("JT") Adams.

———◆———

Q. Hopkinsville-born blues performer John Brim formed what group in the late 1940s?

A. John Brim and his Gary Kings.

Q. During the 1920s what Kentuckian appeared in such New York musical productions as *The Priceless Funny Revue, Brunettes Preferred,* and *Sitting Pretty?*

A. Rosa ("Rose") Henderson.

———◆———

Q. Noted blues singer Helen Humes started her singing career as a child in what Louisville church choir?

A. North Street Baptist Church.

———◆———

Q. What Kentuckian had a gospel music superhit with his recording of "Peace in the Valley"?

A. Red Foley.

———◆———

Q. Olive Hill is the birthplace of what country music composer/singer?

A. Tom T. Hall.

———◆———

Q. Folk/blues performer Bill ("Colonel") Williams was a long-time resident of what Kentucky town?

A. Greenup.

———◆———

Q. Early in his career Stringbean worked with what group at radio station WLAP in Lexington?

A. Cy Rogers' Lonesome Pine Fiddlers.

———◆———

Q. What are the actual names of Naomi and Wynonna Judd?

A. Diana Ellen Judd and Christina Claire Ciminella.

Q. What town is the site of the Kentucky Apple Festival that features apple delicacies, country music, rides, and antique auto and Corvette shows?

A. Paintsville.

———◆———

Q. What Kentuckian appeared in such New York musical revues as *Hot Rhythm, Shuffle Along of 1933, Hummin' Sam,* and *Hot Harlem*?

A. Edith Wilson.

———◆———

Q. Gospel music singing, a parade, and fireworks are all a part of what June event in Manchester?

A. Halleluia.

———◆———

Q. What banjo-picking comic was born in Annville on June 17, 1915?

A. Stringbean.

———◆———

Q. Where is the Great American Brass Bands Festival held?

A. Danville.

———◆———

Q. What Kentuckian penned the Tennessee Ernie Ford hit "Sixteen Tons"?

A. Merle Travis.

———◆———

Q. What was the only commercial recording by Aunt Mollie Jackson, who was born in Clay County in 1880?

A. "Kentucky Miner's Wife."

Q. What long-time member of the Grand Ole Opry and "Hee Haw" was born in Niagara on October 20, 1913?

A. Grandpa Jones.

Q. What is the name of Jamestown's July celebration?

A. Lakefest.

Q. Where is the Official Kentucky State Championship Old Time Fiddlers Contest held?

A. Rough River Dam State Resort Park.

Q. Who supplied the original radio voice of Matt Dillon on "Gunsmoke"?

A. William Conrad.

Q. Appearing on NBC from September 26, 1957, to June 19, 1958, Rosemary Clooney used what theme song on her television show sponsored by Lux soap?

A. "Tenderly."

Q. Henry Hull played what movie role in both *Jesse James* and *The Return of Frank James*?

A. Major Rufus Todd.

Q. What Kentucky native composed and recorded such songs as "Money, Marbles, and Chalk" and "Don't Rob Another Man's Castle" in the late 1940s?

A. Bob Atcher.

Q. Una Merkel was born in what town on December 10, 1903?

A. Covington.

———◆———

Q. The Osborne Brothers left MGM in 1963 to joined what record label?

A. Decca.

———◆———

Q. In what hit bluegrass composition did Bill Monroe immortalize his uncle Pendleton Vandiver?

A. "Uncle Pen."

———◆———

Q. What town is host to the annual Jackson County Rondayvoo celebration?

A. McKee.

———◆———

Q. Character actor Charles Middleton was born in what town on October 3, 1878?

A. Elizabethtown.

———◆———

Q. In 1939 Martha Carson and her sisters joined what all-girl band at radio station WLAP in Lexington?

A. The Sunshine Sisters.

———◆———

Q. What spring event at Harrodsburg features a parade, egg hunt, and entertainment for all ages?

A. Easter Eggstravaganza.

Q. Who played Red Skelton's sidekick Sylvester in MGM's *Whistling in the Dark* (1941), *Whistling in Dixie* (1942), and *Whistling in Brooklyn* (1943)?

A. Rags Ragland.

———◆———

Q. What Kentuckian appeared in such movies as *Requiem for a Heavyweight, The Greatest,* and *Body and Soul?*

A. Muhammad Ali.

———◆———

Q. Dating back to the early 1940s, what summer gospel singing event is held at the Renfro Valley Country Music Center?

A. All-Night Gospel Sing.

———◆———

Q. What event is billed as the largest free music festival in the nation?

A. Louisville Bluegrass & American MusicFest.

———◆———

Q. For whom did Ricky Skaggs play guitar and sing backup from 1977 to 1980?

A. Emmylou Harris.

———◆———

Q. What Louisville-born actress/dancer appeared in *Cold Turkey, Where Lillies Bloom, A Thousand Clowns,* and *They Might Be Giants?*

A. Sudie Bond.

———◆———

Q. What Kentuckian produced musical scores for the movies *The Catman of Paris, Gay Blades, Flame of the Barbary Coast,* and *Night Train to Memphis?*

A. R. Dale Butts.

Q. Where was singer Rosemary Clooney born May 23, 1928?

A. Maysville.

—◆—

Q. Una Merkel made her screen debut in what 1920 movie?

A. *Way Down East*.

—◆—

Q. Where is the Boone County Bluegrass Festival held?

A. Burlington.

—◆—

Q. Cave City is the site of what July gospel music event?

A. Ohio Valley Gospel Sing.

—◆—

Q. What archfiend did Charles Middleton play in three *Flash Gordon* serials?

A. Ming the Merciless.

—◆—

Q. In 1960 what became the first song to break into the record charts for Loretta Lynn?

A. "Honky Tonk Girl."

—◆—

Q. The music style known as "bluegrass" derived its name from what Bill Monroe band?

A. The Bluegrass Boys.

Q. What Kentuckian starred in the television series "Cannon" and "Jake and the Fat Man"?

A. William Conrad.

———◆———

Q. The grounds of what historic home are the site of the Richmond May Festival?

A. Irvinton Mansion.

———◆———

Q. What Kentuckian is known for such country hits as "Lady Lay Down," "Backside of Thirty," and "Common Man"?

A. John Conlee.

———◆———

Q. Rollin and John Sullivan of Edmonton formed what hit country music duo?

A. Lonzo and Oscar.

———◆———

Q. What movie, the second screen appearance for Irene Dunne, became the first western to receive a Best Picture Oscar?

A. *Cimarron.*

———◆———

Q. Tom Ewell won a Tony in 1953 for his performance in what stage production?

A. *The Seven-Year Itch.*

———◆———

Q. Martha Carson and her two sisters joined the Renfro Valley Barn Dance in 1940 to play with what string band?

A. The Coon Creek Girls.

Q. What old-fashioned homecoming celebration is held each May at Silver Grove?

A. Silverfest.

———◆———

Q. Where is the Bluegrass Express Clogging Championship held?

A. Winchester.

———◆———

Q. What film actor from Corbin appeared in *On with the Show, Midshipman Jack,* and *Sixteen Fathoms*?

A. Arthur Lake.

———◆———

Q. In the mid-1970s J. D. Crowe recruited Ricky Skaggs, Tony Rice, and Jerry Douglas to form what country/bluegrass group?

A. New South.

———◆———

Q. What Kentucky-born actor starred opposite Hedy Lamarr in Cecil B. DeMille's 1949 *Samson and Delilah*?

A. Victor Mature.

———◆———

Q. Where was actor Warren Oates born in 1928?
A. Depoy.

———◆———

Q. What Campbellsville's Fourth of July celebration annually draws over 20,000 participants?

A. Independence Appreciation Day.

Q. Each July what Renfro Valley Country Music Center event features over twenty bluegrass and old-time country music groups?

A. Joe Clark Bluegrass Festival.

———◆———

Q. Where is movie director D. W. Griffith buried?

A. Mount Tabor Cemetery at La Grange.

———◆———

Q. Cliff Carlisle was one of the first country performers to play what type of instrument on stage?

A. Dobro guitar.

———◆———

Q. Where was Skeeter Davis born on December 30, 1931?

A. Dry Ridge.

———◆———

Q. Vicki Hackman of Louisville was an original member of what country trio?

A. Dave and Sugar.

———◆———

Q. What was the Duke of Paducah's actual name?

A. Benjamin Francis Ford.

———◆———

Q. Country cooking and gospel music, along with mule and tractor pulls, are all a part of what Madisonville festivity?

A. Mule Day.

Q. Movie director John Carpenter grew up in what community?

A. Bowling Green.

———◆———

Q. The Kentucky HeadHunters evolved out of what earlier group?

A. The Itchy Brothers.

———◆———

Q. Louisville's Leo Burmester made his movie debut in what 1980 thriller?

A. *Cruising*.

———◆———

Q. What celebration is held each May at Menifee?

A. Menifee Mountain Memories Festival.

———◆———

Q. What was the most popular record and theme song of the Coon Creek Girls?

A. "You're a Flower That Is Blooming There for Me."

———◆———

Q. What Kentucky native appeared in such comic movies as *The Great Dictator* and *His Girl Friday*?

A. Billy Gilbert.

———◆———

Q. What celebration is held around Labor Day weekend at Tompkinsville?

A. Monroe County Watermelon Festival.

Q. Patricia Neal made her Broadway debut in what production?

A. *Another Part of the Forest.*

Q. Where did television actor Lee Majors attend college?

A. Eastern Kentucky University.

Q. Kentucky-born actor Ned Beatty appeared in what 1972 adventure thriller?

A. *Deliverance.*

Q. What celebration featuring square dancing, country music, old-fashioned games, and a $10,000 fishing contest is held the first week in July at Morgantown?

A. Green River Catfish Festival.

Q. Actor Tom Cruise attended what Louisville elementary school?

A. St. Raphael Elementary School.

Q. What Muhlenberg County town is known for its annual Fall Music Festival?

A. Central City.

Q. J. D. Crowe formed what bluegrass group in the mid-1960s?

A. The Kentucky Mountain Boys.

Q. Fulton, Hickman, Ballard, and Carlisle counties band together in celebrating what May event?

A. Great River Road Festival.

Q. What Kentucky-born performer originated the "singing news" routine?

A. Lazy Jim Day.

Q. In 1965 William Conrad produced and directed what two movies?

A. *My Blood Runs Cold* and *Brainstorm*.

Q. What amusement park is situated at Cave City?

A. Guntown Mountain.

Q. Top regional artists perform Appalachian folk music at what October musical event at Berea?

A. Celebration of Traditional Music.

Q. What Louisville-born actor played a mad scientist in the 1935 movie *The Werewolf of London*?

A. Henry Hull.

Q. What was motion picture director D. W. Griffith's full name?

A. David Wark Griffith.

Q. Billed as America's favorite outdoor musical, *The Stephen Foster Story* is performed in what city?

A. Bardstown.

———◆———

Q. What movie from Louisville producer Jerry Lee Rodgers was filmed in Jefferson County in 1981?

A. *Springfield Coach.*

———◆———

Q. In 1970 what became the first record to chart for Crystal Gayle?

A. "I Cried (the Blue Right Out of My Eyes)."

———◆———

Q. What old-fashioned festivity is held each October in Grayson?

A. Carter County Sorghum Festival.

———◆———

Q. What Kentucky-born cinematographer received Oscars for his work on *King Solomon's Mines, The Bad and the Beautiful,* and *Ben Hur*?

A. Robert Surtees.

———◆———

Q. In what community is the Breathitt County Honey Festival held?

A. Jackson.

———◆———

Q. What long-time pastor of the First Baptist Church in Morehead was best known in folk and mountain music circles for "The Waggoner Sod"?

A. Buell Kazee.

Q. Mary Frances Penick is the actual name of what Kentucky-born country music singer?

A. Skeeter Davis.

———◆———

Q. What member of the McLain Family Band has served as a professor of music at Berea College?

A. Raymond McLain.

———◆———

Q. The Western Square Dance Festival is held at which state park?

A. Natural Bridge State Resort Park.

———◆———

Q. Kentucky-born jazz musician Horacee Arnold formed what group in the 1960s?

A. The Here and Now Company.

———◆———

Q. With what Kentuckian did Conway Twitty team up to record such country hits as "Louisiana Woman, Mississippi Man" and "As Soon As I Hang Up the Phone"?

A. Loretta Lynn.

———◆———

Q. What unique celebration is held each September at Battletown?

A. The Pepper Festival.

———◆———

Q. In 1968 the Happy Goodman Family was awarded a Best Gospel Performance Grammy for what album?

A. *The Happy Gospel of the Happy Goodman Family.*

HISTORY

Q. What notorious outlaw, along with his four gang members, robbed the Southern Bank in Russellville of nine thousand dollars on March 20, 1868?

A. Jesse James.

———◆———

Q. On what date did Kentucky become a state?

A. June 1, 1792.

———◆———

Q. What was Kentucky's first television station, which opened in Louisville in 1948?

A. WAVE–TV.

———◆———

Q. How much was James Taylor paid in 1795 for land on which to erect Campbell County's first courthouse?

A. One shilling.

———◆———

Q. How many men involved in the French-Eversol feud were killed in the Hazard County courthouse shoot-out of 1888?

A. Twelve.

Q. What one-time Cynthiana resident served as special U.S. commissioner to Germany, Hungary, and Switzerland in the mid-1800s?

A. Ambrose Dudley Mann.

———◆———

Q. The Kentucky Colonization Society sent how many freed slaves to Liberia in March 1833?

A. 102.

———◆———

Q. What military engagement on January 10, 1862, prevented Confederate troops from advancing up the Big Sandy Valley to the Ohio River?

A. The battle of Middle Creek.

———◆———

Q. How much did Stephen Giles Letcher and Benjamin Letcher charge to construct Garrard County's first courthouse in 1798?

A. 410 pounds.

———◆———

Q. According to tradition, what adventurer, along with his companions, removed large quantities of silver from eastern Kentucky between 1760 and 1769?

A. John Swift.

———◆———

Q. Starting in 1921, the Newport steelworkers' strike lasted for how many years?

A. Seven.

———◆———

Q. In 1789, who founded the first settlement in Lawrence County between the forks of the Big Sandy River?

A. Charles Vancouver.

Q. At its peak during the early- and mid-1800s, Gen. Thomas Kennedy's plantation near Paint Lick covered how many acres?

A. 15,000.

Q. Who founded Newport in 1790?

A. Hubbard Taylor.

Q. In 1839 what Washington native became secretary of war of the Republic of Texas?

A. Albert Sidney Johnston.

Q. In what year was the railroad extended from Lexington to Jackson?

A. 1890.

Q. What future U.S. president commanded a brigade of Union troops at the battle of Middle Creek?

A. James A. Garfield.

Q. Founded in 1787, what was the first fort in the Big Sandy Valley?

A. Harmon's Station.

Q. What Lancaster resident served as chief justice of the Kentucky Court of Appeals from 1810 to 1826?

A. John Boyle.

Q. William Kennedy, along with other prominent northern Kentucky citizens, founded what educational facility in 1798?

A. Newport Academy.

———◆———

Q. In 1970 what Glasgow native joined President Richard Nixon's administrative staff as assistant to the deputy press secretary?

A. Diane Sawyer.

———◆———

Q. Who made a survey in 1773 of the land where Louisville now stands?

A. Capt. Thomas Bullitt.

———◆———

Q. What employee of the Ohio Land Company became the first white man to visit Big Bone Lick in March 1751?

A. Christopher Gist.

———◆———

Q. What Kentuckian served as secretary of war under President Franklin Pierce?

A. Jefferson Davis.

———◆———

Q. In what years did Lazarus W. Powell serve as governor of Kentucky?

A. 1851 to 1855.

———◆———

Q. What name was given early Kentucky frontier hunters who spent long periods of time pursuing game in the wilds?

A. Long hunters.

Q. Who issued a proclamation in 1763 forbidding settlers to move west of the Appalachian highland watershed?

A. King George III of England.

———◆———

Q. As an Indian captive, who became the first white woman to visit the Kentucky region?

A. Mary Inglis.

———◆———

Q. What document, signed on February 10, 1763, relinquished French land holdings east of the Mississippi River to the English?

A. Treaty of Paris.

———◆———

Q. In what year was the settlement of Boonesboro begun?

A. 1775.

———◆———

Q. What English poet made the legendary hero Daniel Boone a worldwide figure by devoting seven stanzas to him in a long romantic poem?

A. Lord Byron ("Don Juan," 1823).

———◆———

Q. As a result of lobbying by slave holders, men of what profession were prohibited from serving as lawmakers under Kentucky's second constitution?

A. Ministers.

———◆———

Q. How many divisions comprised the bill of rights attached to Kentucky's first constitution?

A. Twenty-seven.

Q. Who became the first governor of Kentucky on June 4, 1792?

A. Gen. Isaac Shelby.

———◆———

Q. In 1930 what percentage of Kentucky's population was classified as urban?

A. 30.6 percent.

———◆———

Q. What two Kentuckians received a Congressional Medal of Honor for heroism during World War I?

A. Samuel Woodfill and Willie Sandlin.

———◆———

Q. What was the population of Kentucky in 1790?

A. 73,677.

———◆———

Q. Who served as governor of Kentucky from 1804 to 1808?

A. Christopher Greenup.

———◆———

Q. How many Kentuckians served in the military during World War I?

A. 75,043.

———◆———

Q. What was the length of the wooden covered bridge constructed across the Kentucky River south of Nicholasville in 1838?

A. 240 feet.

Q. At the beginning of the Civil War, approximately how many slaves were there in Kentucky?

A. 225,000.

———◆———

Q. What was the population of Hazard in 1910?

A. 537.

———◆———

Q. In 1861 what became the first Federal recruiting station to be established south of the Ohio River?

A. Camp Dick Robinson.

———◆———

Q. What noted Kentucky political figure was admitted to the bar of the Quarter Sessions Court at Cynthiana in 1801?

A. Henry Clay.

———◆———

Q. Who selected the site for Fort Thomas in 1887?

A. Gen. Philip H. Sheridan.

———◆———

Q. Henry Smith, who served as the provisional governor of Texas in 1824 and 1837–38 was born in what Bryantsville road house?

A. Burnt Tavern.

———◆———

Q. Cynthiana was captured by what Confederate general in both 1862 and 1864?

A. John H. Morgan.

Q. Erected near Nicholasville in 1782, what is believed to have been the first grist mill in the state?

A. Glass's Mill.

———◆———

Q. For what purpose did Union forces during the Civil War use the original building of the First Baptist Church in Paducah?

A. As a hospital.

———◆———

Q. In whose administration did Kentuckian Alben W. Barkley serve as vice president of the United States?

A. Harry S Truman.

———◆———

Q. Organized in 1832, what is Paducah's oldest church congregation?

A. Broadway United Methodist Church.

———◆———

Q. At whose home near Bardstown was the Confederate flag first raised over Kentucky?

A. William E. Johnson.

———◆———

Q. During the 1820s what was the price of a meal complete with whiskey at Bright's Inn near Stanford?

A. Twenty-five cents.

———◆———

Q. Situated between Rowland and Brodhead, what structure, built around 1785, is said to be the first brick house built in Kentucky?

A. The Col. William Whitley home.

Q. What Somerset resident was the governor of Kentucky from 1919 to 1923?

A. Edwin P. Morrow.

———◆———

Q. On what date was Abraham Lincoln born in Hardin County?

A. February 12, 1809.

———◆———

Q. In 1827 what Englishman purchased the Elmwood Hall estate at Ludlow hoping to establish a utopian city to be called Hygeia?

A. William Bullock.

———◆———

Q. Under whose command did 15,000 Union soldiers construct the defenses which became known as Fort Mitchell?

A. Gen. Lew Wallace.

———◆———

Q. In what year was Georgetown College established?

A. 1829.

———◆———

Q. What famous Mingo chief was killed during an attack on McClelland's Station in Scott County in December 1776?

A. Chief Pluggy.

———◆———

Q. In what structure was Madison County's first court session held in 1778?

A. Col. John Miller's barn.

Q. What 1874 college campus was the forerunner of Eastern Kentucky University?

A. Central University.

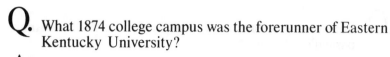

Q. At what landmark did the battle of Richmond start in 1862?

A. Mount Zion Church.

Q. What institution of higher learning was founded in Madison County in 1853?

A. Berea College.

Q. What Mount Vernon structure dating back to 1790 served as a station on the Underground Railroad?

A. Langford House.

Q. The Methodist Episcopal Church established what institution of higher learning at London in 1896?

A. Sue Bennett College.

Q. How many pioneers were killed or taken captive at the 1784 Defeated Camp Massacre on Little Laurel River?

A. Thirty-seven.

Q. Who blazed a trail in 1775 that became known as the Wilderness Road?

A. Daniel Boone.

Q. For what pioneer and Indian fighter was Williamsburg named?

A. Col. William Whitley.

———◆———

Q. With the first settlers arriving in 1889, what was the population of Middlesboro by the end of 1890?

A. Ten thousand.

———◆———

Q. What was the name of Isaac Shelby's home near Junction City?

A. Traveler's Rest.

———◆———

Q. What Farmington native served as U.S. attorney general under Abraham Lincoln?

A. James Speed.

———◆———

Q. What Trappist monastery was founded near New Haven in 1848?

A. Abbey of Our Lady of Gethsemane.

———◆———

Q. In 1904 what state historical treasure was stored in the basement of the Poffenhaufen mansion at College Point on Long Island, New York?

A. Abraham Lincoln's birthplace cabin.

———◆———

Q. What was the make and model of Paducah's first motorized fire truck?

A. 1913 LaFrance.

Q. Constructed in the late 1700s, what Bardstown facility is said to be the oldest inn in continuous operation west of the Alleghenies?

A. Old Talbott Tavern.

Q. What former Revolutionary War general was the first lawyer to practice in Glasgow?

A. Alexander E. Spottswood.

Q. In 1936 what facility did the Department of the Treasury construct at Fort Knox?

A. The Gold Bullion Depository.

Q. Who became Abraham Lincoln's stepmother in 1819?

A. Sarah Bush Johnston.

Q. What three other states besides Kentucky are officially called *Commonwealths*?

A. Massachusetts, Pennsylvania, and Virginia.

Q. What nickname was given to the Confederate First Kentucky Cavalry operating outside of its free-state home?

A. Orphan Brigade.

Q. What one-time resident of Elizabethtown served as the territorial governor of Florida from 1822 to 1834?

A. W. P. Duvall.

Q. What Elizabethtown lawyer served as the territorial governor of Illinois from 1809 to 1818?

A. Ninian Edwards.

———◆———

Q. Confederate brigadier general Ben Hardin of Elizabethtown was offered what position in the Union army at the outbreak of the Civil War?

A. Paymaster.

———◆———

Q. What colorful Civil War general and western Indian fighter was a resident of Elizabethtown from 1871 to 1873?

A. George Armstrong Custer.

———◆———

Q. What Hart County native and former Confederate general was a candidate for the U.S. vice presidency in 1896?

A. Simon Bolivar Buckner.

———◆———

Q. How many Union soldiers were captured by Confederate general Braxton Bragg on September 17, 1863, at the battle of Munfordville?

A. Four thousand.

———◆———

Q. In 1813 the General Assembly established what school at Bowling Green?

A. Warren Seminary.

———◆———

Q. Where did Confederate cavalryman John Morgan and his men hide from Federal troops following the burning of the Shakertown depot?

A. Lost River Cave.

Q. On July 22, 1806, what notorious outlaw was killed and his head displayed on a pole in Webster County?

A. Micajah ("Big") Harpe.

———◆———

Q. What church denomination established Augusta College in 1799?

A. Methodist.

———◆———

Q. Who donated land to Hopkins County in 1797 to bring the county seat to the evolving community of Hopkinsville?

A. Bartholomew Wood.

———◆———

Q. What U.S. president grew up and is buried just northeast of Louisville?

A. Zachary Taylor.

———◆———

Q. Within one month of their arrival at Camp Beauregard near Mayfield in November 1861, how many Confederate troops died from illness?

A. Fifteen hundred.

———◆———

Q. What Washington resident was appointed the territorial governor of Iowa in 1841 by President William Henry Harrison?

A. John Chambers.

———◆———

Q. In 1785 who became surveyor general of Kentucky?

A. Col. Thomas Marshall.

Q. What Revolutionary War soldier settled Powersville around 1783?

A. Capt. Philip Buckner.

———◆———

Q. Around 1822 what famous educator and textbook developer taught school at Paris?

A. William Holmes McGuffey.

———◆———

Q. In 1804 what new Protestant denomination was established by Rev. Barton W. Stone at Cane Ridge in Bourbon County?

A. Christian Church.

———◆———

Q. Dr. J. W. Hughes established what school at Wilmore in 1890?

A. Asbury College.

———◆———

Q. In 1805 what Quaker sect established a community in Mercer County?

A. Shakers.

———◆———

Q. To whom was Sarah Taylor, daughter of Zachary Taylor, married?

A. Jefferson Davis (his first wife).

———◆———

Q. In 1855, what Carrollton native declined an appointment to serve as territorial governor of Nebraska?

A. William Orlando Butler.

Q. What fortification was constructed at Stamping Ground in 1790?

A. Lindsey's Stockade.

Q. Prior to his death in 1850, who is said to have owned 40 percent of all land in Shelby and Henry counties?

A. Thomas Smith.

Q. Who laid the cornerstone for the Lincoln Memorial in 1909?

A. Former President Theodore Roosevelt.

Q. On September 6, 1871, who became the first former Confederate to be named to the Kentucky Court of Appeals after the Civil War?

A. Judge W. S. Pryor.

Q. What large railroad corporation moved its headquarters to Anchorage in 1916?

A. Southern Pacific Railroad.

Q. Who founded the Kentucky Military Institute near Lyndon in 1845?

A. Robert T. P. Allen.

Q. How many prisoners were electrocuted at the state penitentiary at Eddyville between 1911 and 1935?

A. Eighty-four.

Q. What fortification was constructed near present-day Wickliffe in 1780 by Gen. George Rogers Clark?

A. Fort Jefferson.

———◆———

Q. How many Confederate cannon were placed on the bluffs near Columbus to control traffic on the Mississippi River?

A. 140.

———◆———

Q. What legendary railroad man was born at Jordan on March 14, 1864?

A. John Luther ("Casey") Jones.

———◆———

Q. Who settled Hickman in 1819?

A. James Mills.

———◆———

Q. What company purchased the Maysville and Big Sandy Railroad in 1888?

A. C. and O. Railroad.

———◆———

Q. What pioneer Baptist minister, noted for bringing the Traveling Church from Virginia to Kentucky in 1781, is buried at Minerva?

A. Lewis Craig.

———◆———

Q. As a boy what U.S. president attended the Rand and Richardson School at Maysville for one year?

A. Ulysses S. Grant.

Q. A granite marker was erected in 1925 near Washington to commemorate what frontiersman and the stockade he built in the area?

A. Simon Kenton.

———◆———

Q. In whose home did the first Mason County court convene on May 26, 1789?

A. Robert Rankins.

———◆———

Q. What Kentuckian was given charge of the Confederate Army of the West in 1861?

A. Albert Sidney Johnston.

———◆———

Q. Who was the first surveyor of Kenton County?
A. John May.

———◆———

Q. What bloody engagement on August 19, 1782, ended the Revolutionary War in the West?

A. Battle of Blue Licks.

———◆———

Q. Thomas Metcalfe, Kentucky's tenth governor, was known by what nickname?

A. Old Stone Hammer.

———◆———

Q. Erected in 1804, what was the first hotel in Paris?
A. The Indian Queen.

Q. Of the participants in the legendary and long-running Hatfield–McCoy feud, which family was based in Kentucky, with the other clan in West Virginia?

A. McCoy clan.

———◆———

Q. Indians under the leadership of what chief attacked Harrodburg in 1777?

A. Chief Blackfish.

———◆———

Q. Who was Kentucky's last surviving Shaker who died in 1925 at age eighty-seven?

A. Sister Mary Settles.

———◆———

Q. Who was selected in 1861 to serve as the Confederate provisional governor of Kentucky?

A. George W. Johnson.

———◆———

Q. What black school was established in 1904 after the state legislature banned integration at Berea College?

A. Lincoln Institute.

———◆———

Q. Who served as president of Transylvania University from 1818 to 1829?

A. Dr. Horace Holley.

———◆———

Q. William Hardin, who in 1780 constructed the fort around which Hardinsburg grew, was known to the Indians by what nickname?

A. Big Bill.

Q. What title was given to the conflict between members and nonmembers of the Tobacco Growers' Association in the early 1900s?

A. The Tobacco War (Black Patch War).

———◆———

Q. In what year was the State Highway Commission created?

A. 1912.

———◆———

Q. What four camps were established in Kentucky to train troops during World War I?

A. Knox, Thomas, Zachary Taylor, and Stanley.

———◆———

Q. In 1895 who became Kentucky's first Republican governor?

A. William O. Bradley.

———◆———

Q. The Kentucky General Assembly passed what law on March 15, 1894, that gave women property rights in conjunction with their husbands?

A. Weissenger Act.

———◆———

Q. In 1817 what two turnpike road companies were chartered in the state?

A. Lexington–Maysville and Lexington–Louisville.

———◆———

Q. What law was passed by the Kentucky legislature during World War I to insure that every able-bodied man supported the war effort?

A. "Work or Fight" law.

Q. In Kentucky's early history what year was known as the "Bloody Year"?

A. 1780.

Q. In what year was the Governor's Mansion completed?

A. 1914.

Q. What Kentuckian became the first American soldier to die in France in World War I?

A. Samuel M. Wilson.

Q. How many days did it take the *Enterprise* in 1817 to become the first steamboat to ascend the Mississippi and Ohio rivers from New Orleans to Louisville?

A. Twenty-five.

Q. What Lexington resident bequeathed $60,000 to Transylvania University in 1823?

A. Col. James Morrison.

Q. In addition to 421 flatboats and keelboats, how many steamboats passed through the Louisville and Portland Canal in 1831?

A. 406.

Q. What Kentuckian was appointed ambassador to Mexico by President Zachary Taylor?

A. Robert P. Letcher.

Q. On January 29, 1835, how long did it take the first train to travel from Lexington to Frankfort?

A. Two hours, twenty-nine minutes.

———◆———

Q. What Kentuckian was elected vice president of the United States in 1836?

A. Richard M. Johnson.

———◆———

Q. On what date was the first rail of the Lexington and Ohio Railroad laid?

A. October 22, 1830.

———◆———

Q. What act by the state government on January 29, 1830, provided for the first tax-supported schools in Kentucky?

A. Common-school Law.

———◆———

Q. What could not be legally imported into Kentucky after February 1833?

A. Slaves.

———◆———

Q. On February 5, 1842, what state facility for the visually handicapped was established in Louisville?

A. Kentucky Institute for the Blind.

———◆———

Q. What religious denomination was formed in Louisville in May 1845?

A. Methodist Episcopal Church, South (Southern Methodist Church).

Q. Whose body was brought from Missouri and re-interred at Frankfort Cemetery on September 13, 1845?

A. Daniel Boone.

———◆———

Q. Where was the first wire suspension railroad bridge to span the Kentucky River completed on July 19, 1851?

A. Frankfort.

———◆———

Q. On May 18, 1853, what steamboat reached Louisville from New Orleans in a record time of four days, nine hours, and thirty-one minutes?

A. *Eclipse.*

———◆———

Q. How many people died in Louisville during the "Bloody Monday" election day riots of 1855?

A. Twenty-two.

———◆———

Q. What Kentuckian joined President Abraham Lincoln's cabinet as postmaster general on March 5, 1861?

A. Montgomery Blair.

———◆———

Q. Clay City was the site of what early-nineteenth century blast furnace and forge?

A. Red River Iron Works.

———◆———

Q. In what year was Newport incorporated as a city?
A. 1835.

Q. Arriving in 1673, who was probably the first Englishman on Kentucky soil?

A. Gabriel Arthur.

Q. The Bank of Kentucky was organized in 1806 with what amount of authorized capital?

A. One million dollars.

Q. Where did the first black high school in the state open on October 7, 1873?

A. Louisville.

Q. What Louisa native became chief justice of the U.S. Supreme Court in 1946?

A. Fred Vinson.

Q. How many pounds of gunpowder did George Rogers Clark secure from the government officials of Virginia in 1776 for the protection of the Kentucky region?

A. Five hundred.

Q. In what year was Kentucky's second constitution adopted?

A. 1799.

Q. Who was twice brought to trial in the federal court of the District of Kentucky on treason charges in the early 1800s?

A. Aaron Burr.

Q. What Kentuckian was a candidate for U.S. president in 1824?

A. Henry Clay.

———◆———

Q. Under Kentucky's first constitution, suffrage was limited to what group of citizens?

A. White males age twenty-one and over.

———◆———

Q. In what year was Kentucky's first telephone exchange put into service in Louisville?

A. 1879.

———◆———

Q. How old was John Crepps Wickliffe Beckham when he was sworn in as the governor of Kentucky on February 3, 1900?

A. Thirty-one.

———◆———

Q. In 1922 what Louisville radio station became the first commercial station in the state?

A. WHAS.

———◆———

Q. In 1852 what Kentuckian presented a bill to Congress requesting that George Washington's birthday be made a national holiday?

A. John J. Crittenden.

———◆———

Q. What state law passed in 1908 helped establish rights for children?

A. Child Labor Law.

Q. In August 1867 who was elected state superintendent of public schools in Kentucky?

A. Zachariah F. Smith.

———◆———

Q. How many churches were there in Kentucky when statehood was granted?

A. Forty-two (with 3,095 members).

———◆———

Q. On what date did the Louisville and Nashville Railroad inaugurate its first rail service?

A. November 1, 1859.

———◆———

Q. Approximately how many Kentuckians over the age of twenty were unable to read in 1840?

A. 42,000.

———◆———

Q. In 1928 what property was purchased by Louisville for a commercial airport?

A. Bowman Field.

———◆———

Q. During the formation of the Missouri Compromise what Kentuckian became known as the "Great Compromiser" and the "Great Pacificator"?

A. Henry Clay.

———◆———

Q. On December 13, 1983, who was sworn in as Kentucky's first woman governor?

A. Martha Layne Collins.

Q. What Henderson schoolteacher started observing Mother's Day in 1887?

A. Mary Towles Sassen Wilson.

———◆———

Q. Who was the founder and promoter of Kentucky Fried Chicken?

A. Col. Harland Sanders.

———◆———

Q. What Georgetown resident in 1789 fermented and distilled a mixture of corn, rye, and barley malt to produce the state's first bourbon whiskey?

A. Rev. Elijah Craig.

———◆———

Q. What former member of the U.S. House of Representatives and Senate and governor of Kentucky, had two sons, both generals, fighting in opposing forces at the battle of Shiloh?

A. John J. Crittenden.

———◆———

Q. Who was governor of Kentucky during the Great Depression of the 1930s?

A. Ruby Laffoon.

———◆———

Q. To what was the voting age lowered in Kentucky in 1955?
A. Eighteen.

———◆———

Q. What Democratic candidate for governor was shot by an assassin on January 30, 1900?

A. William Goebel.

Q. In 1972 the state legislature passed its first tax on the production of what commodity?

A. Coal.

------◆------

Q. In what year did the Kentucky Turnpike between Louisville and Elizabethtown open?

A. 1956.

------◆------

Q. Dan Carter Beard, who spent his childhood in Covington, founded what organization for boys in the United States?

A. The Boy Scouts of America.

------◆------

Q. What Frankfort resident was the first United States senator from Kentucky?

A. John Brown.

------◆------

Q. In what year was Louisville incorporated as a city?
A. 1828.

------◆------

Q. What religious seminary moved to Louisville in 1877 from Greenville, South Carolina?

A. Southern Baptist Theological Seminary.

------◆------

Q. Who was the only Know-Nothing party candidate to be elected as governor of Kentucky?

A. Charles S. Morehead (1855–1859).

ARTS & LITERATURE

CHAPTER FOUR

Q. What artist best known for his *Birds of America* lived in Henderson and Louisville for several years?

A. John James Audubon.

———◆———

Q. On what date was Kentucky's first newspaper printed?

A. August 11, 1787.

———◆———

Q. In 1853 what Louisville resident became the first black to publish a novel in the United States?

A. William Wells.

———◆———

Q. The Kentucky Renaissance Festival is held in what community?

A. Shelbyville.

———◆———

Q. In 1962 what two writers collaborated to produce *Kentucky Yesterday and Today*?

A. Ruby Dell Baugher and Sarah Hendricks Claypool.

Q. What is the only resident professional theater between Louisville and Nashville?

A. Horse Cave Theatre.

———◆———

Q. Jesse Hilton Stuart, who achieved literary fame in 1934 with his *Man with a Bull-Tongue Plow,* was born near what community?

A. Riverton.

———◆———

Q. What native Kentucky artist of the late 1700s and early 1800s was called the "best painter west of the Appalachians"?

A. Matthew H. Jouett.

———◆———

Q. A mob of southern sympathizers destroyed the office and equipment of what Newport newspaper in 1856?

A. *True South.*

———◆———

Q. What Kentuckian is said to have been the inspiration for the character of Little Eva in Harriet Beecher Stowe's *Uncle Tom's Cabin?*

A. Nancy Kennedy Letcher.

———◆———

Q. Housed in a renovated 1939 art deco movie theater, what is the name of Bowling Green's art center?

A. Capitol Arts Center.

———◆———

Q. What novelist served as associate editor at the Louisville *Times* from 1945 to 1950?

A. Augusta Wallace Lyons.

Q. What 1818 Bardstown residence was the inspiration for Stephen Foster's "My Old Kentucky Home"?

A. Federal Hill Manor.

———◆———

Q. In what year was the Paducah Boys Choir founded?

A. 1977.

———◆———

Q. What was the title of Kentucky-born Muhammad Ali's 1975 autobiography?

A. *The Greatest: My Own Story.*

———◆———

Q. Where was author, humorist, and lecturer Irvin S. Cobb born?

A. Paducah.

———◆———

Q. In what city may one visit the Houchens Art Gallery?

A. Bowling Green.

———◆———

Q. The *Guardian of Liberty* was what Kentucky town's first newspaper?

A. Cynthiana.

———◆———

Q. What artist, who relocated to the Pine Mountain area in 1962, became famous for his water fowl and wildlife studies?

A. Ray Harm.

Q. What Kentuckian wrote the classic college textbook *A Study of Jazz*?

A. Paul Tanner.

———◆———

Q. Country music composer Troy Seals was born in what Kentucky community on November 16, 1938?

A. Big Hill.

———◆———

Q. What Louisville-born screenwriter produced scripts for such movies as *Three Coins in a Fountain, The Teahouse of the August Moon,* and *The World of Suzie Wong*?

A. John Patrick.

———◆———

Q. The drama *The Sword of Kentucky* is based on what historical character?

A. Gen. George Rogers Clark.

———◆———

Q. What Pippa Passes grocery store and gas station owner started her writing career after she was past sixty?

A. Verna May Slone.

———◆———

Q. In 1928 the John Reed Memorial Prize for poetry was awarded to what Perryville native?

A. Elizabeth Madox Roberts.

———◆———

Q. What was the first newspaper to be published in Kentucky?

A. *Kentucky Gazette*, Lexington.

Q. Gracey-born silent film actress-writer Sara Barker Strayer used what pen name?

A. Margery Wilson.

———◆———

Q. The University of Kentucky features 300 dancers along with guest artists at what spring event?

A. American College Dance Festival.

———◆———

Q. What 1980 autobiography was about country music star Loretta Lynn?

A. *Coal Miner's Daughter.*

———◆———

Q. What Kentuckian was full-time assistant on President Nixon's memoirs?

A. Diane Sawyer.

———◆———

Q. Noted primarily for beautiful landscapes, painter Russell May was born in what Kentucky town?

A. Prestonsburg.

———◆———

Q. What east Kentucky creek's name is a corruption of a place-name from *Gulliver's Travels*?

A. Lulbegrud (from Lorbrulgrud).

———◆———

Q. Such poetry collections as *Fringes of Sky, Skip to My Lou, My Darling,* and *Petals from the Dogwood Tree* are the works of what Kentucky native?

A. Elisabeth Offutt Allen.

Q. Who established the *Kentucky Herald*, the state's second newspaper, in Lexington in 1793?

A. James H. Stewart.

Q. Poet Juliet Hoyt Alves, who is noted for her works of the 1930s and 1940s, was born in what town?

A. Henderson.

Q. Librarian and folklorist Janet Alm Anderson wrote what 1986 nonfiction book about the Bluegrass state?

A. *A Taste of Kentucky*.

Q. Louisville hosts what annual theatrical event featuring new works?

A. Humana Festival of New American Plays.

Q. Cale Young Rice, who wrote numerous collections of poetry and plays, was born in what community in 1872?

A. Dixon.

Q. How old was Louisville poet Amelia B. Welby when her *Poems by Amelia* was published in 1845?

A. Sixteen.

Q. What Lexington artist illustrated Washington Irving's *The Pride of the Village* and *Annette Delabre*?

A. William Edward West.

Q. Professional storytellers spin yarns and ghost stories at what Nelson County spring event?

A. Historic Bardstown Storytelling Festival.

———◆———

Q. In the 1860s, what well-known fiction writer was brought as an infant to Lexington where her father was the rector of Christ Church Episcopal?

A. Mary Shipman Andrews.

———◆———

Q. Established and edited by Shadrach Penn in 1818, what was Louisville's first newspaper?

A. The *Advertiser*.

———◆———

Q. What highly acclaimed author, who was born in Wayne County, published *The Dollmaker* in 1954?

A. Harriette S. Arnow.

———◆———

Q. Jan Arnow, who served as executive director of the Art Center in Louisville, produced what 1984 nonfiction work?

A. *Louisville Slugger: The Making of a Baseball Bat.*

———◆———

Q. Where was poet Sylvia T. Auxier born in 1900?
A. McAndrews.

———◆———

Q. In 1832 what painter, best known for his portraits of U.S. presidents, moved to Louisville?

A. James Reid Lambdin.

Q. Who brought the first theatrical troupe of any consequence to Kentucky in December 1815?

A. Samuel Drake.

———◆———

Q. *Bowling Green: A Pictorial History* was compiled in 1983 by what Kentucky librarian?

A. Nancy Disher Baird.

———◆———

Q. Cherokee Triangle Olde Time Arts & Crafts Fair is held in what city?

A. Louisville.

———◆———

Q. Who compiled *A History of Scott County As Told by Its Buildings* in 1981?

A. Ann Bolton Bevins.

———◆———

Q. Where was author and educator Abraham Flexner born in 1866?

A. Louisville.

———◆———

Q. What educational facility sponsors the Chamber Music Celebration, featuring both amateur and professional musicians?

A. Morehead State University.

———◆———

Q. What newspaper sympathetic to the Whig party was established in Louisville in November 1830?

A. The *Journal.*

Q. What Frankfort-born fiction writer penned *The Good Time Gospel Boys* in 1987?

A. Billy Bittinger.

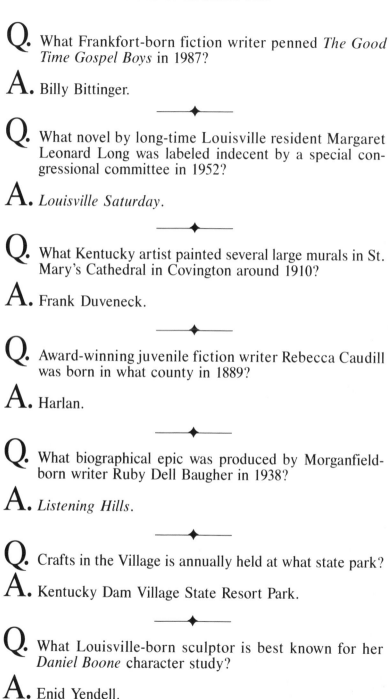

Q. What novel by long-time Louisville resident Margaret Leonard Long was labeled indecent by a special congressional committee in 1952?

A. *Louisville Saturday.*

Q. What Kentucky artist painted several large murals in St. Mary's Cathedral in Covington around 1910?

A. Frank Duveneck.

Q. Award-winning juvenile fiction writer Rebecca Caudill was born in what county in 1889?

A. Harlan.

Q. What biographical epic was produced by Morganfield-born writer Ruby Dell Baugher in 1938?

A. *Listening Hills.*

Q. Crafts in the Village is annually held at what state park?

A. Kentucky Dam Village State Resort Park.

Q. What Louisville-born sculptor is best known for her *Daniel Boone* character study?

A. Enid Yendell.

Q. What Franklin native served as state librarian and penned *Woman in Politics*?

A. Emma Guy Cromwell.

———◆———

Q. Olive Tilford Dargan, who penned such dramas as *Lords and Lovers* and *The Woods of Ida,* was born in what town in 1870?

A. Tilfordsville.

———◆———

Q. What community sponsors the Otter Creek Storytelling Festival?

A. Vine Grove.

———◆———

Q. In 1844 what newspaperman established the *Courier* in Louisville?

A. Walter N. Haldeman.

———◆———

Q. What Bowling Green author wrote about Mimi and her adventures in Mammoth Cave and other Kentucky sites?

A. Anne Penee Davis.

———◆———

Q. In what year was folk performer, composer, and poet John Jacob Niles born in the Portland neighborhood of Louisville?

A. 1892.

———◆———

Q. What outdoor drama facility is situated at Caneyville?

A. Pine Knob Theater.

Q. Novelist Jude Devereaux grew up in what Kentucky community?

A. Fairdale.

———◆———

Q. *The Egyptian Elements in the Legend of the Body and Soul* was penned by what Georgetown-born writer and educator?

A. Louise Dudley.

———◆———

Q. In 1983 Phyllis George Brown authored what nonfiction title?

A. *The I Love America Diet.*

———◆———

Q. To what county did author Janice Holt Giles relocate in 1949?

A. Adair.

———◆———

Q. In what year was Louisville's theatrical event, *Classics in Context,* begun at Actors Theatre?

A. 1985.

———◆———

Q. What Lexington-born author wrote the 1979 fictional work *Sleepless Nights*?

A. Elizabeth Hardwick.

———◆———

Q. Where is the Salt River Storytelling Festival held?

A. Shepherdsville.

Q. Where is the Norton Center for the Arts?

A. Centre College, Danville.

———————◆———————

Q. What Louisville author wrote scripts for "Rhoda" and several other television shows?

A. Sue Grafton.

———————◆———————

Q. The movie *Gorillas in the Mist* was based on the life of what writer who had worked as an occupational therapist in Kentucky from 1955 to 1966?

A. Dian Fossey.

———————◆———————

Q. Growing up in Louisville as Mary Lee King, what journalist wrote the 1977 biography *The Life and Loves of Cary Grant*?

A. Lee Guthrie.

———————◆———————

Q. The Shaker Festival, hosted by South Union in Logan County, features what outdoor musical drama?

A. *Shakertown Revisited.*

———————◆———————

Q. What newspaper did James Guthrie found in Louisville in 1844?

A. The *Democrat.*

———————◆———————

Q. At what facility does Berea host the Kentucky Guild of Artists & Craftsmen's Spring Fair?

A. Indian Fort Theatre.

Q. What theatrical group performs at Pewee Valley?

A. The Little Colonel Players.

———◆———

Q. Shelbyville-born author Fannie Calpwell Macaulay wrote under what pseudonym?

A. Frances Little.

———◆———

Q. Award-winning author Isabel McLennan McMeekin was born in what city in 1895?

A. Louisville.

———◆———

Q. What historical drama about the life of Cassius Marcellus Clay is performed at the White Hall State Historic Site?

A. *The Lion of White Hall.*

———◆———

Q. *Murder in Prospect, Kentucky* was penned by what Kentucky native in 1967?

A. Augusta Wallace Lyons.

———◆———

Q. What lifelong Kentucky resident was called the "Dean of Louisville Writers"?

A. George Madden Martin.

———◆———

Q. The 1966 collection of short stories *Ready for the Ha Ha & Other Stories* was written by what Louisville native?

A. Jane Mayhall.

Q. What Louisville newspapermen received the 1980 Pulitzer Prize for international reporting?

A. Joel Brinkley and Jay Mather.

---◆---

Q. Jazz educator Paul Tanner was born in what community on October 15, 1917?

A. Skunk Hollow.

---◆---

Q. What summer event at Harrodsburg features visual and fine arts, dance, mime, photography, music, and drama?

A. Express Y'self/Arts on Main.

---◆---

Q. What Louisville *Times* editorial cartoonist won a 1956 Pulitzer prize?

A. Robert York.

---◆---

Q. "Storytelling in a Cave" takes place in what geologically formed theatre?

A. Cascade Cave, Carter Caves State Resort Park.

---◆---

Q. What Auburn-born writer has written several books on the Shakers?

A. Julia Neal.

---◆---

Q. Prestonsburg is the home of what outdoor theater?

A. Jenny Wiley Theatre.

Q. What Louisville native wrote the biography *Dolly* in 1978 and *Talking with the Legends of Country Music* in 1985?

A. Alanna Nash.

———◆———

Q. What novels did Eleanor Mercein Kelly write with a Kentucky setting?

A. *The Mansion House* and *Kildares of Storm*.

———◆———

Q. In what year was Louisville's old three-story brick City Theater destroyed by fire?

A. 1843.

———◆———

Q. What folk composer, arranger, collector, and performer has been called the "Dean of American balladeers"?

A. John Jacob Niles.

———◆———

Q. Main Street on Stage, featuring puppet shows, storytelling, and dance, is held in what Trigg County community?

A. Cadiz.

———◆———

Q. Louisville native Marsha Norman received a Pulitzer Prize for drama for what 1983 work?

A. *'night, Mother*.

———◆———

Q. During the summer, where is the historical drama *The Legend of Daniel Boone* performed?

A. Old Fort Harrod State Park.

Q. What was the only published work by Princeton-born novelist Frances Ogilvie?

A. *Green Bondage.*

---◆---

Q. Short story writer and novelist Eliza Calvert Obenchain was born and spent most of her life in what community?

A. Bowling Green.

---◆---

Q. What community is the home of the Historic Heritage House Dinner Theatre?

A. Fort Knox.

---◆---

Q. In what year did Walter N. Haldeman found the Louisville *Times*?

A. 1884.

---◆---

Q. Where does the Central Kentucky Concert Band perform?

A. Haggin Auditorium, Transylvania University.

---◆---

Q. Published in 1901, what was the first book by Shelbyville native Alice Hegan Rice?

A. *Mrs. Wiggs of the Cabbage Patch.*

---◆---

Q. What Viper-born writer and musician wrote several books on Appalachian music and the dulcimer?

A. Jean Ritchie.

Q. Where is the Fresh Air Arts Fair held?

A. Shillito Park, Lexington.

———◆———

Q. What Lexington-born jazz musician's photographic works were exhibited at the Studio Museum of Harlan?

A. Les McCann.

———◆———

Q. The American Folk Song Society was founded by what Kentucky folklorist?

A. Jeannette ("Jean") Bell Thomas.

———◆———

Q. The 1911 performances of what theatrical group ushered in the "little theater" movement in Kentucky?

A. University of Louisville Players.

———◆———

Q. What Lexington author produced fifteen biographies for young readers during the 1950s and 1960s?

A. Katharine Elliott Wilkie.

———◆———

Q. Who established the Owensboro *Messenger* in 1881?

A. Urey Woodson.

———◆———

Q. Kentucky-born drama critic John Mason Brown wrote what book in 1929?

A. *The Modern Theatre in Revolt.*

Q. *The Thread That Runs So True,* an autobiographical account of school teaching in the Kentucky mountains, was written by what novelist and poet?

A. Jesse Stuart.

———◆———

Q. Published in 1887, what was the title of Louisville poet Madison Cawein's first collection of works?

A. *Blooms of the Berry.*

———◆———

Q. What world famous architect designed the city hall in Paducah?

A. Edward Durrell.

———◆———

Q. Where is the Horse Cave Theatre housed?

A. Thomas Opera House.

———◆———

Q. Whitesburg is the site of what spring tribute to Appalachian music and storytelling?

A. Seed Time on the Cumberland.

———◆———

Q. Jackson Purchase Arts & Crafts Festival is held at what outdoor site?

A. Kenlake State Resort Park.

———◆———

Q. Black poet Joseph Seaman Cotter founded what school in Louisville?

A. Samuel Coleridge-Taylor School.

Q. In the late 1800s and early 1900s what long-time resident of Pewee Valley created the popular Little Colonel series of books?

A. Annie Fellows Johnston.

———◆———

Q. Where is the Kentucky Shakespeare Festival held?

A. Central Park, Louisville.

———◆———

Q. What lively Morgantown musical depicts life in a turn-of-the-century community on the Green River?

A. *The Magic Belle*.

———◆———

Q. At which university is the Price-Doyle Fine Arts Center?

A. Murray State University.

———◆———

Q. Who was the first newspaperman in Kentucky?

A. John Bradford.

———◆———

Q. What Kentucky juvenile fiction writer is known for such works as *Happy Little Family, Tree of Freedom, Time for Lissa,* and *Contrary Jenkins*?

A. Rebecca Caudill.

———◆———

Q. Grayson County native Olive Tilford Dargan sometimes used what pen name?

A. Fielding Burke.

Q. In 1870 what became Lexington's first daily newspaper?

A. The *Press*.

———◆———

Q. What drama critic, born in Louisville in 1900, was frequently published in the New York *Evening Post* and *The Saturday Review*?

A. John Mason Brown.

———◆———

Q. The Paducah Art Guild Gallery is housed in what historic downtown facility?

A. Market House.

———◆———

Q. Stage and theater manager Samuel Drake died on his farm in what county on October 16, 1854?

A. Oldham.

———◆———

Q. What Guthrie-born novelist, poet, and literary critic won the 1947 Pulitzer Prize for fiction for *All the King's Men*?

A. Robert Penn Warren.

———◆———

Q. In the early 1800s, artisans Asa Blanchard and Samuel Ayres were best known for their work in what material?

A. Silver.

———◆———

Q. In 1825 what city was considered the cultural and arts center of Kentucky?

A. Lexington.

Q. What painter settled in Georgetown about 1840?

A. E. F. Goodard.

———◆———

Q. Author John Fox, Jr., known for his best-selling *The Little Shepherd of Kingdom Come* and *The Trail of the Lonesome Pine,* was born in what town?

A. Paris.

———◆———

Q. What Winchester-born sculptor is best known for his *Triumph of Chastity* and his statue of Henry Clay?

A. Joel T. Hart.

———◆———

Q. In what county was black poet Joseph Seaman Cotter born in 1861?

A. Nelson.

———◆———

Q. What 1947 novel by Louisville author Gwen Davenport was made into the movie *Sitting Pretty*?

A. *Belvedere.*

———◆———

Q. From Irvin S. Cobb's humorous stories, what became his most popular character?

A. Judge Priest.

———◆———

Q. What was the title of Jesse Stuart's autobiography, published in 1938?

A. *Beyond Dark Hills.*

Q. What author, born in Lexington in 1849, became known for such works as *A Kentucky Cardinal, The Choir Invisible,* and *The Reign of Law?*

A. James Lane Allen.

Q. Who built a new $200,000 theater bearing his name in Louisville in 1873?

A. Barney Macanley.

Q. What Kentucky painter has been called "the Audubon of the flower set"?

A. Nellie Meadows.

Q. The 1984 autobiography *Grandpa: 50 Years Behind the Mule* is based on the life of what entertainer?

A. Grandpa Jones.

Q. Held each year in Lexington, what is the largest theatrical event in central Kentucky?

A. Shakespeare Festival in Woodland Park.

Q. What Kentucky artist created the *Kentucky Wilderness* series of paintings?

A. Alan K. Cornett.

Q. During the late 1800s and early 1900s what Kentucky poet was called "the Keats of the South"?

A. Madison Cawein.

SPORTS & LEISURE

C H A P T E R   F I V E

Q. What was the distance of the Kentucky Derby prior to its shortening to one and one-fourth miles in 1896?

A. One and one-half miles.

———◆———

Q. Where was long-time Western Kentucky basketball coach Edgar ("Ed") Diddle born on March 12, 1895?

A. Gradyville.

———◆———

Q. What Murray State air riflist was a gold medal winner at the 1984 Olympics in Los Angeles?

A. Pat Spurgin.

———◆———

Q. In 1902 what Louisville Colonel led the AA in batting with a .370 percentage?

A. John Ganzel.

———◆———

Q. What were the athletic team colors at the University of Kentucky prior to the adoption of blue and white in 1892?

A. Blue and light yellow.

Q. The Lady Colonels is the nickname of what Kentucky university women's basketball team?

A. Eastern Kentucky University.

———◆———

Q. In the 1989 NBA draft what University of Louisville player was the first-round, first pick of Sacramento?

A. Pervis Ellison.

———◆———

Q. What black sprinter from Lexington was a member of the 1912 U.S. Olympic team?

A. Howard Drew.

———◆———

Q. Ellis Johnson produced how many Little All-Americans in football at Morehead State?

A. Nine.

———◆———

Q. In what year was organized football first played at Eastern Kentucky University?

A. 1909.

———◆———

Q. What University of Kentucky record setting number of free throws were made by Kenny Walker during the 1984–85 season?

A. 218.

———◆———

Q. Who became coach of the Lady Kats in 1987?

A. Sharon Fanning.

Q. On July 23, 1919, Brooklyn Dodger (Pee Wee) Reese was born in what Kentucky town?

A. Ekron.

———◆———

Q. In 1970 John Bover set a Murray State University outdoor record by hurling a javelin what distance?

A. 231 feet, 9 inches.

———◆———

Q. Westley Unseld played basketball at what Louisville high school?

A. Seneca High School.

———◆———

Q. What is the oldest country club in McCracken County?

A. Paducah Country Club.

———◆———

Q. How many points did Eastern Kentucky University score in 1986 to set an OVC record for most points scored kicking during a single season?

A. Eighty-seven.

———◆———

Q. What basketball player, born in Smith Mills, is considered to be the first to use the modern jump shot?

A. John Cooper.

———◆———

Q. What two baseball clubs offered contracts to college basketball and football great Wallace ("Wah-Wah") Jones?

A. Chicago White Sox and Boston Braves.

Q. After graduating from Western Kentucky University, with what basketball team did Bobby Rascoe play in 1963–66?

A. Phillips 66ers.

———◆———

Q. When is the Kentucky Derby run each year?

A. First Saturday in May.

———◆———

Q. What nickname was given Paducah-born NAIA Hall of Fame basketball coach Clarence Gaines?

A. Big House.

———◆———

Q. How many seasons did E. A. Diddle coach basketball at Western Kentucky University?

A. Forty-two (1922–64).

———◆———

Q. Where was former heavyweight boxing champion Muhammad Ali born on January 18, 1942?

A. Louisville.

———◆———

Q. Although Murray State University's Stewart Johnson went on to play all nine years of his pro career in the ABA, what NBA team first drafted him in 1966?

A. New York Knicks.

———◆———

Q. In 1966 what football player set a University of Louisville season record with fifty-nine receptions?

A. Jim Zamberlan.

Q. How many three-point field goals did Western Kentucky University's Brett McNeal sink during the 1989-90 season?

A. Seventy-five.

———◆———

Q. What nickname was given to Murray State University's six-foot, nine-inch basketball player Stewart Johnson?

A. Big Stew.

———◆———

Q. Johnny Unitas was the ninth-round draft pick of what pro team in 1955?

A. Pittsburgh Steelers.

———◆———

Q. On July 19, 1924, what Louisville-born pitcher became the last person in the National League to throw and win two complete games on the same day?

A. Herman S. Bell.

———◆———

Q. What year was Pat Riley voted All-American?

A. 1966.

———◆———

Q. Following his career at Murray State University, Jeff Martin signed with what NBA team in 1989?

A. Los Angeles Clippers.

———◆———

Q. Johnny Unitas passed for how many touchdowns during his University of Louisville career?

A. Twenty-seven.

Q. The University of Kentucky's swim teams are known by what name?

A. Katfish.

---◆---

Q. Eastern Kentucky University won its first national football crown in 1979 by defeating what school 30–7?

A. Lehigh.

---◆---

Q. What is the name of the St. Louis Cardinals' Triple-A farm team?

A. Louisville Redbirds.

---◆---

Q. How many NCAA Championships did the University of Louisville basketball teams capture during the 1980s?

A. Two (1980 and 1986).

---◆---

Q. What was Bennie Purcell's now-retired Murray State University jersey number?

A. 21.

---◆---

Q. A statue of what famous race horse is situated at the entrance of Kentucky Horse Park?

A. Man o' War.

---◆---

Q. What 100-acre site at Cadiz offers softball fields, baseball fields, a horse show ring, a motorcycle track, and hiking trails?

A. Trigg County Recreation Complex.

Q. What was Muhammad Ali's name prior to his embracing the Black Muslim religion in 1964?

A. Cassius Marcellus Clay.

◆

Q. In 1967 what Western Kentucky University football player ranked first in the NCAA with 1,444 yards in nine games?

A. Dickie Moore.

◆

Q. What 1990 national championship did the Lady Kats capture?

A. National Women's Invitational Tournament.

◆

Q. In 1968 what University of Louisville basketball player was Baltimore's first-round, second pick in the NBA draft?

A. Wes Unseld.

◆

Q. Who became head track and cross-country coach at Eastern Kentucky University in 1979?

A. Rick Erdmann.

◆

Q. What epidemic led to the cancellation of University of Kentucky football during the 1918 season?

A. Influenza.

◆

Q. How many points did Darrell Griffith score during his 1976–80 career at the University of Louisville?

A. 2,333.

Q. What Clark County native became coach of the women's tennis team at Western Kentucky University in 1985?

A. Ray Rose.

———◆———

Q. Serving from 1946 to 1962, who was Eastern Kentucky University's winningest basketball coach?

A. Paul McBrayer.

———◆———

Q. What University of Louisville player was named Most Valuable Offensive Player at the 1991 Fiesta Bowl?

A. Browning Nagle.

———◆———

Q. Who set a single game Western Kentucky University record in 1978 with five touchdown passes against Morehead State?

A. Leo Peckenpaugh.

———◆———

Q. What 1911–13 University of Kentucky football player later gained fame with the St. Louis Browns by pitching the first home-run ball to Babe Ruth?

A. Jim Park.

———◆———

Q. Who did Eastern Kentucky University defeat in 1982 to capture its second national football championship?

A. Delaware (17–14).

———◆———

Q. Who is credited with bringing football to the University of Kentucky?

A. Professor A. M. Miller.

Q. Who set a Murray State University record with thirty-three consecutive free throws during the 1989-90 season?

A. Greg Coble.

———◆———

Q. What was the University of Louisville's 1990 football season record, noted as the best of its history?

A. 10–1–1.

———◆———

Q. What are the athletic team colors for Eastern Kentucky University?

A. Maroon and white.

———◆———

Q. With what national baseball organization was Louisville affiliated between 1902 and 1962?

A. American Association.

———◆———

Q. Where did Bill Curry coach just prior to joining the University of Kentucky as head football coach for the 1990 season?

A. Alabama.

———◆———

Q. In 1984, with a career total of 1,920 points, who became the all-time scoring leader for the Eastern Kentucky University Lady Colonels?

A. Lisa Goodin.

———◆———

Q. What basketball team is at home in Rupp Arena?

A. University of Kentucky Wildcats.

Q. The University of Louisville defeated what team, 34–20, at the Sun Bowl, January 1, 1958?

A. Drake.

———◆———

Q. Alex Groza, Ralph Beard, Kenny Rollins, Wah Wah Jones, and Cliff Barker were known by what title during the 1947–48 University of Kentucky basketball season?

A. The Fabulous Five.

———◆———

Q. Who joined Eastern Kentucky University's staff in 1988 as head coach of the women's basketball team?

A. Larry Joe Inman.

———◆———

Q. During the 1920 pennant race, what Liberty-born Yankees pitcher fatally struck Beaver Dam-born Ray Chapman of the Indians with a fast ball?

A. Carl May.

———◆———

Q. What University of Kentucky basketball player made a 52.5-foot shot against Tennessee in 1948?

A. Ralph Beard.

———◆———

Q. Who did Western Kentucky University defeat, 34–19, in the 1952 Refrigerator Bowl?

A. Arkansas State.

———◆———

Q. Where was pitcher Woodrow Thompson ("Woodie") Fryman born in 1940?

A. Ewing.

Q. What is the mascot/symbol for Eastern Kentucky University sporting events?

A. The Colonel (old southern gentleman).

———◆———

Q. Dan Swartz, Morehead State basketball star of the 1950s, was given what nickname?

A. Dogpatch.

———◆———

Q. What Pebworth native coached the Yankees in 1935–44, the Browns in 1947, and the Red Sox in 1948–52?

A. Earl Bryan Combs.

———◆———

Q. On March 26, 1949, what basketball team did the University of Kentucky defeat 46–36, to win their second straight NCAA championship?

A. Oklahoma.

———◆———

Q. Against what team did Kentuckian James Paul David Bunning pitch a perfect game on June 21, 1964?

A. New York Mets.

———◆———

Q. What Eastern Kentucky University player was voted NFL Defensive Rookie of the Year in 1973 with the Chicago Bears?

A. Wally Chambers.

———◆———

Q. Who holds the University of Kentucky record for most personal fouls during a three-season period?

A. Pat Riley (294, 1965–67).

Q. What year did the University of Kentucky add women's swimming to its competitive sports?

A. 1983.

———◆———

Q. What has been the home arena for Eastern Kentucky University women's basketball since 1976?

A. Paul S. McBrayer Arena.

———◆———

Q. Kathy DeBoer, University of Kentucky head volleyball coach, received what prestigious award in 1987?

A. National Coach of the Year.

———◆———

Q. What volleyball player set a University of Kentucky career record in 1985–88 with 1,657 kills?

A. Lisa Bokovoy.

———◆———

Q. In 1982 Laura Linder set a University of Kentucky season record for an individual volleyball player with how many assists?

A. 1,477.

———◆———

Q. What diving and swimming facility was opened at the University of Kentucky on March 29, 1989?

A. Harry C. Lancaster Aquatic Center.

———◆———

Q. What basketball player set an Eastern Kentucky University career scoring record between 1983 and 1987 with a total of 1,723 points?

A. Antonio Parris.

Q. University of Louisville swimming star Wynn Paul introduced what aquatic competitive sport to the University of Kentucky as head swimming coach?

A. Water polo.

———◆———

Q. In 1936 the title "dry land swimming team" was applied to what university's men's swimming team because the school did not have a pool?

A. University of Kentucky.

———◆———

Q. What is the name of the University of Kentucky women's basketball team?

A. Lady Kats.

———◆———

Q. In what year did Murray State University's women's volleyball team capture its first OVC championship?

A. 1989.

———◆———

Q. What is the home court of the Lady Kats?

A. Memorial Coliseum.

———◆———

Q. In what year did Eastern Kentucky University have its first undefeated football team during a regular season?

A. 1940.

———◆———

Q. What Eastern Kentucky University staff member was selected the OVC's Golf Coach of the Year in 1984, 1985, and 1986?

A. Lew Smither.

Q. By what name were Valerie Still, Patty Jo Hedges, and Lea Wise of the 1983 Lady Kats basketball team known?

A. The Terrific Trio.

———◆———

Q. On December 1, 1984, who accepted the job offer to become the head football coach at the University of Louisville?

A. Howard Schnellenberger.

———◆———

Q. Who set a career scoring record with the Lady Kats in 1979–83 with 2,763 points?

A. Valerie Still.

———◆———

Q. What team did the University of Louisville tie in the 1970 Pasadena Bowl?

A. Long Beach State.

———◆———

Q. In 1968, with what time did Jim Green set a University of Kentucky men's outdoor record for the 100 meters?

A. 10.0 seconds.

———◆———

Q. While at Western Kentucky University, how many points did Lillie Mason score for the Lady Toppers?

A. 2,262.

———◆———

Q. What Louisville-born swimmer won three gold medals at the 1984 Olympics in Los Angeles?

A. Mary T. Meagher.

Q. Ranked as the nation's oldest continually running horse racing event, when was the Kentucky Derby first run?

A. 1875.

───────◆───────

Q. Who set the University of Kentucky women's records in discus and shot-put in 1981, and javelin in 1982?

A. Cindy Crapper.

───────◆───────

Q. What university's athletic teams are called the Hilltoppers?

A. Western Kentucky University.

───────◆───────

Q. What horse racing facility is at Franklin?

A. Dueling Grounds Race Course.

───────◆───────

Q. During 1985–88 Jay Gruden set a University of Louisville career record with how many touchdown passes?

A. Forty-four.

───────◆───────

Q. What is the earliest recorded date for cross-country racing as a sport at the University of Kentucky?

A. 1912.

───────◆───────

Q. In 1978 Pat Chimes set a Murray State University record for an outdoor mile with what time?

A. 4:01.7.

Q. For what two years did Western Kentucky University's Carlyle Towery receive All-American honors in basketball?

A. 1940 and 1941.

＋

Q. During the 1989–90 season who became the sixth Lady Colonel in the history of Eastern Kentucky University to surpass the 1,000-point career scoring mark as a junior?

A. Kelly Cowan.

＋

Q. In 1973 what new time record did Secretariat establish at the Kentucky Derby?

A. 1 minute, 59⅖ seconds.

＋

Q. What Lynch-born basketball player was named All-American in 1947?

A. Leland Byrd.

＋

Q. University of Louisville football coach Howard Schnellenberger coached what pro team in 1973–1974?

A. Baltimore Colts.

＋

Q. The 1926 basketball All-American Carey ("Blue") Burgess attended what Lexington high school?

A. Henry Clay High School.

＋

Q. In 1925 what football coach led the University of Louisville to an 8–0 winning season?

A. Tom King.

Q. In what year did the University of Kentucky participate in its first nationally televised football game?

A. 1956 (against Georgia Tech).

———◆———

Q. What years did Johnny Unitas play at the University of Louisville?

A. 1951-54.

———◆———

Q. Warren County-born Darel Carrier averaged how many points per game during his basketball career at Western Kentucky University in 1962–64?

A. 19.1.

———◆———

Q. What ABA team did Darel Carrier join upon leaving Western Kentucky University?

A. Kentucky Colonels.

———◆———

Q. Eastern Kentucky University's George Floyd set an OVC individual career record with how many pass interceptions from 1978 to 1981?

A. Twenty-two.

———◆———

Q. What Newport-born basketball player led the NBA for his first year in pro play with 350 fouls?

A. Dave Cowens.

———◆———

Q. In 1952 what Western Kentucky University quarterback became All-American?

A. Jimmy Feix.

Q. Who became head basketball coach at Eastern Kentucky University in 1989?

A. Mike Pollio.

Q. During his 1933–35 career at the University of Kentucky, quarterback Norris McMillan was known by what nickname?

A. OO.

Q. What Slat-born basketball player was a three-time NAIA All-American and two-time AAU All-American?

A. Ken Davis.

Q. In 1986 who became the head coach of the Lady Toppers' golf program at Western Kentucky University?

A. Kathy Teichert.

Q. Neon-born basketball player Johnny Cox was named All-SEC for what three years?

A. 1957, 1958, and 1959.

Q. What University of Louisville player made sixteen free throws against Notre Dame on December 22, 1956?

A. Charlie Tyra.

Q. Where was two-time All-Missouri Valley and 1960 All-American basketball player Everett Dean born?

A. Vanceburg.

Q. What Walton-born basketball player was credited as being the first to use the one-hand overhead pivot shot?

A. John ("Frenchy") DeMoisey.

———◆———

Q. Who became the first person in basketball coaching history to coach one thousand games at one college?

A. Edgar ("Ed") Diddle.

———◆———

Q. What Berea native was selected as a member of the 1956 U.S. Olympic basketball team?

A. Billy Evans.

———◆———

Q. What University of Kentucky coach was relieved of his responsibilities during the 1926 season, only to have the players go on strike and force his return?

A. Fred J. Murphy.

———◆———

Q. What organization was formed to encourage, support, and promote the intercollegiate baseball program at Eastern Kentucky University?

A. The EKU Diamond Boosters.

———◆———

Q. In the 1947 season what Murray State basketball player became the first scoring sensation in the pros?

A. Joe ("Jumping Joe") Fulks.

———◆———

Q. What facility is home to the University of Louisville's football team?

A. Cardinal Stadium.

Q. What are the athletic team colors at the University of Louisville?

A. Red, black, and white.

Q. How many University of Kentucky head football coaches lettered in football for the Wildcats?

A. Four (J. W. Guyn, A. D. Kirwan, Charlie Bradshaw, and Jerry Claiborne).

Q. What Western Kentucky guard was selected Ohio Valley Player of the Year in 1965, 1966, and 1967?

A. Clem Haskins.

Q. What University of Louisville coach was inducted into the UCLA Athletic Hall of Fame in 1990?

A. Denny Crum.

Q. By what pro basketball team was Campbellsville-born player Clem Haskins drafted in 1967?

A. Chicago Bulls.

Q. What Owensboro native and NBA player with St. Louis from 1957 to 1966 was nicknamed Li'l Abner?

A. Cliff Hagan.

Q. Born in Owingsville, Vern Hatton played basketball at what Lexington high school before being named All-SEC twice in his collegiate career?

A. Lafayette High School.

Q. Lenny Lyles set a University of Louisville season record in 1957 with how many rushing touchdowns?

A. Seventeen.

———◆———

Q. What Louisville native was named to the All-Time Sugar Bowl team?

A. Lee Huber.

———◆———

Q. Who was the first basketball player to score points for Adolph Rupp at the University of Kentucky?

A. Ellis Johnson.

———◆———

Q. What Eastern Kentucky University athlete was the 1988 Ohio Valley Conference individual cross-country champion?

A. David Hawes.

———◆———

Q. In what year did Denny Crum become the seventeenth head basketball coach at the University of Louisville?

A. 1971.

———◆———

Q. Because of an inability to pronounce his first name, who gave Wallace Jones his nickname Wah-Wah?

A. His younger sister Jackie.

———◆———

Q. In 1969 who set a Louisville city basketball prep record with an average 27.1 points per game?

A. Ron King.

Q. Who is the winningest coach in the history of Eastern Kentucky University football?

A. Roy Kidd.

Q. What Louisville-born basketball player was All-Big 7 in 1956, 1957, and 1958 while playing for Kansas State?

A. Jack Parr.

Q. What Eastern Kentucky University player kicked an OVC record sixty-two-yard field goal against Murray State in 1986?

A. Paul Hickert.

Q. Jeff Mullins, who played in the NBA with the Hawks, Warriors, and Bulls, was born in what Kentucky city?

A. Lexington.

Q. What was Johnny Unitas's jersey number at the University of Louisville?

A. 19.

Q. Who was head basketball coach at the University of Kentucky from 1973 to 1985?

A. Joe B. Hall.

Q. What ABA Kentucky Colonels coach was born in Corydon?

A. Frank Ramsey.

Q. Between 1965 and 1968, what player set an Eastern Kentucky University career record with 5,041 yards passing?

A. Jim Guice.

———◆———

Q. Who served as head fooball coach at the University of Louisville from 1946 to 1968?

A. Frank Camp.

———◆———

Q. The United States was represented by what Murray State University air riflist in the 1988 Olympics?

A. Deena Wigger.

———◆———

Q. What Western Kentucky basketball player was All-Ohio Valley in 1960, 1961, and 1962?

A. Bobby Rascoe.

———◆———

Q. In what year did the University of Kentucky football team first begin to travel by air?

A. 1946.

———◆———

Q. With a season total of eight, in what year did Eastern Kentucky University suffer its most defeats in football?

A. 1929.

———◆———

Q. Who started in the 1914–15 season as Western Kentucky University's first head basketball coach?

A. J. L. Arthur.

Q. Arnold Risen, who played pro basketball with Indianapolis, Rochester, and Boston during the 1940s and 1950s, was born in what Kentucky community?

A. Williamstown.

Q. Who became head coach of women's volleyball at Murray State University in 1987?

A. Oscar Segovia.

Q. What former University of Kentucky basketball forward was elected to the state House of Representatives in 1971?

A. Forest Sale.

Q. Frank Selvy, who twice led the nation in scoring in college basketball, was born in what town in 1932?

A. Cordin.

Q. Who was "Mr. Basketball" in Kentucky and was a prep All-American in 1962?

A. Mike Silliman.

Q. How many times was Louisville-born basketball player Mike Silliman voted All-Army?

A. Four (1967, 1968, 1969, and 1970).

Q. David Russell ("Gus") Bell, who played for the Cincinnati Reds in 1953–61, was born in what Kentucky city on November 15, 1928?

A. Louisville.

Q. What was the nickname of Bernard L. Hickman, the University of Louisville's head basketball coach from 1944 to 1967?

A. Peck.

———◆———

Q. In 1903 who became the first to receive letters in women's basketball at the University of Kentucky?

A. Alice Pence and Christina Pence.

———◆———

Q. What Western Kentucky forward was Ohio Valley All-Star in 1966–67?

A. Greg Smith.

———◆———

Q. To how many victories did Adolph Rupp coach the Wildcats' basketball team during his 1931-72 career at the University of Kentucky?

A. 875.

———◆———

Q. Dan Swartz, top scorer at Morehead State in 1954–56, later set many team records with what NIBL team?

A. Wichita Vickers.

———◆———

Q. Tom Thacker, who played in the ABA in 1964–68 and the NBA in 1969–71, was born in what town in 1939?

A. Covington.

———◆———

Q. What Lexington native was the first honorary member of the Indiana PGA?

A. Carey Spicer.

Q. With what two NBA teams did University of Louisville basketball star Charles Tyra play in 1958–62?

A. New York and Chicago.

◆

Q. Who was Eastern Kentucky University's first basketball coach, serving 1907–1912?

A. Clyde H. Wilson.

◆

Q. In how many major bowl games did the University of Kentucky participate during the Bear Bryant era?

A. Four: Great Lakes (1947), Orange (1950), Sugar (1951), and Cotton (1952).

◆

Q. In 1935 the black college football National Championship Award was bestowed upon what school by the *Chicago Defender*?

A. Kentucky State College.

◆

Q. What Kentucky tackle was named Most Valuable Player of the 1951 Sugar Bowl?

A. Walt Yowarsky.

◆

Q. To what city did Louisville give up its National League baseball franchise following the 1899 season?

A. Pittsburgh.

◆

Q. What manager led the Louisville Colonels to the 1925 AA pennant?

A. Joe McCarthy.

Q. What 1962 and 1963 basketball letterman at the University of Kentucky became mayor of Lexington?

A. Scotty Baesler.

———◆———

Q. Who started the women's track and field program at Murray State University in 1968?

A. Margaret Simmons.

———◆———

Q. In what year did the Louisville Colonels secure their first AA championship?

A. 1909.

———◆———

Q. In 1930 what two schools defeated Eastern Kentucky University's football team 52–0?

A. University of Louisville and Murray State University.

———◆———

Q. Completed in 1973, what facility replaced Stoll Field as the home of University of Kentucky football?

A. Commonwealth Stadium.

———◆———

Q. What Louisville Colonel set an AA individual season record with 282 hits in 1921?

A. Jay Kirke.

———◆———

Q. In 1921 what school pulled its football team off the field in a call dispute, giving the University of Louisville a forfeit win?

A. Hanover.

Q. In what year was University of Kentucky coach Adolph Rupp inducted into the College Basketball Hall of Fame?

A. 1969.

———◆———

Q. Following his 1924 season with the Louisville Colonels, Earl Bryan Combs signed with what American League team for a reputed $50,000?

A. New York Yankees.

———◆———

Q. Adrian ("Odie") Smith, who was born in Farmington on October 5, 1936, played for what ABA team?

A. Virginia Squires.

———◆———

Q. What three-time All-Indiana Collegiate Conference basketball player was born in Louisville on June 14, 1937?

A. Ed Smallwood.

———◆———

Q. Forest Sale, who was Helms Player of the Year in 1933, derived what nickname from his agricultural studies?

A. Aggie.

———◆———

Q. What is Kentucky-born Pee Wee Reese's full name?

A. Harold H. Reese.

———◆———

Q. Due to lax 1906 rules during World War I, J. White Guyn, Eger Murphree, and John Heber each received how many football letters from the University of Kentucky?

A. Five.

Q. What pro team did Rick Pitino coach prior to joining the University of Kentucky as head basketball coach?

A. New York Knickerbockers.

———◆———

Q. How many victories did Southgate-born pitcher James Paul David Banning secure during his major league career?

A. 224.

———◆———

Q. What jockey rode Aristides to win the first Kentucky Derby?

A. Oliver Lewis.

———◆———

Q. Who set a University of Kentucky basketball single game record by scoring fifty-three points against Mississippi on February 7, 1970?

A. Dan Issel.

———◆———

Q. What St. Louis Cardinals' pitcher of the 1930s was born in Springfield on October 17, 1906?

A. Paul ("Duke") Derringer.

———◆———

Q. On February 23, 1987, whose number 32 Lady Topper jersey was officially retired at Western Kentucky?

A. Lillie Mason.

———◆———

Q. What facility served as home court for University of Kentucky basketball from 1924 to 1950?

A. Alumni Gym.

Q. Jesse Tannehill, who pitched with five major league teams, was born in what town in 1874?

A. Dayton.

———◆———

Q. Wes Unseld set a University of Louisville single game individual scoring record with how many points against Georgetown on December 1, 1967?

A. Forty-five.

———◆———

Q. What major league catcher was born in Paducah on March 5, 1941?

A. Phil Roof.

———◆———

Q. Record-setting hurdler Percy Beard from Hardinsburg was a member of what U.S. Olympic team?

A. 1932.

———◆———

Q. What is the name of the University of Louisville's sports teams?

A. Cardinals.

———◆———

Q. In the pros, what Hazard-born basketball player became known as the Kentucky Rifle?

A. Glen Combs.

———◆———

Q. What was the distance of the long basket shot that the University of Kentucky's Cliff Barker made against Vanderbilt on February 26, 1949?

A. Sixty-three feet, seven inches.

Q. Louisville native Ron Laird competed as a walker on how many U.S. Olympic teams?

A. Three (1960, 1964, and 1968).

———◆———

Q. In 1921 who became the first University of Kentucky basketball player to receive the title of All-American?

A. Basil Hayden.

———◆———

Q. What is the name of the Murray State athletic teams?

A. Racers.

———◆———

Q. Against what opponent did the University of Kentucky basketball team score an SEC single game record of 143 points on February 27, 1956?

A. Georgia.

———◆———

Q. What was Murray State University basketball star Jeff Martin's jersey number?

A. Number 15.

———◆———

Q. In 1912 who became the first head football coach at the University of Louisville?

A. Lester Lawson.

———◆———

Q. What University of Kentucky lineman of the 1916 squad later became governor of the state and a member of the U.S. Senate?

A. Earle Clements.

Q. How many free throws did Murray State University's Howie Crittenden make during the 1953–54 season?

A. 222.

———◆———

Q. A University of Louisville game team record was set with how many dunks against Virginia Tech on February 2, 1990?

A. Twelve.

———◆———

Q. During what season did Murray State University's basketball team have a record twenty-seven wins?

A. 1937–38.

———◆———

Q. What are the colors of the Murray State athletic teams?

A. Blue and gold.

———◆———

Q. Kenny Rollins, University of Kentucky basketball star of the 1940s, had brief careers with what three pro teams?

A. Chicago Stags, Louisville Aluminites, and Boston Celtics.

———◆———

Q. What Wickliffe native, following a career at the University of Louisville, saw NBA service with Philadelphia, Cincinnati, St. Louis, and New York in 1959–61?

A. Phil Rollins.

———◆———

Q. In what year did Jim Ward join Eastern Kentucky University as head baseball coach?

A. 1980.

Q. Murray State University's women's volleyball players set a team record with how many kills against Southeast Missouri State on November 9, 1987?

A. Ninety.

———◆———

Q. What facility preceded Freedom Hall as the home court for University of Louisville basketball?

A. The Armory (now Louisville Gardens).

———◆———

Q. Fred Sowerby, Murray State University track legend of the 1970s, is a native of what country?

A. Antigua.

———◆———

Q. What Eastern Kentucky University staff member was named Ohio Valley Baseball Coach of the Year in 1989?

A. Jim Ward.

———◆———

Q. What was the first season that Bennie Purcell coached men's tennis at Murray State University?

A. 1965–66.

———◆———

Q. In what year did the nickname Wildcats become official at the University of Kentucky?

A. 1911.

———◆———

Q. Who set a Murray State University outdoor shot-put record of fifty-seven feet, seven inches in 1981?

A. Andy Vince.

Q. In what year did the University of Kentucky play its first night football game?

A. 1929.

—————◆—————

Q. In 1979 what became Western Kentucky University's athletic mascot?

A. Big Red.

—————◆—————

Q. Who set a University of Kentucky men's indoor high jump record at seven feet, two and one-quarter inches in 1981?

A. Marvin Mays.

—————◆—————

Q. What is the name of Western Kentucky University's football facility?

A. L. T. Smith Stadium.

—————◆—————

Q. Kentucky-born shortstop Raymond Johnson Chapman stole how many bases in 1917 while with the Cleveland Indians?

A. Fifty-two.

—————◆—————

Q. On what date did Western Kentucky University play its first home football game at night?

A. September 19, 1987.

—————◆—————

Q. Who took over as head football coach at Western Kentucky University on February 1, 1989?

A. Jack Harbaugh.

Q. In what 1963 bowl game did Western Kentucky University defeat Coast Guard 27–0?

A. Tangerine Bowl.

———◆———

Q. Because of their height, what nickname was hung on the University of Kentucky's 1965–66 basketball team?

A. Rupp's Runts.

———◆———

Q. On November 27, 1924, Western Kentucky University's football team defeated what school 73–0?

A. Bethel.

———◆———

Q. In what year was Murray State University's rifle team first recognized as national champions by the National Rifle Association?

A. 1978.

———◆———

Q. With a final tally of 0–1–0, what was Western Kentucky University's worst football season?

A. 1920.

———◆———

Q. What basketball players led the Murray State University Thoroughbreds in 1950–51 to a 21–6 record?

A. Bennie Purcell and Garrett Beshear.

———◆———

Q. In 1975 the University of Louisville basketball program became a charter member of what athletic conference?

A. Metro Conference.

Q. What was the only year Ernie Miller served as head football coach at Western Kentucky University?

A. 1932.

———◆———

Q. Noted Eastern Kentucky University basketball coach Paul McBrayer was born in what community?

A. Lawrenceburg.

———◆———

Q. Western Kentucky's football great Jeff Cesarone attempted how many passes during his 1984–87 career?

A. 1,379.

———◆———

Q. Roy Skinner, who served as head basketball coach at Vanderbilt University in 1961–72, was born in what Kentucky city on April 17, 1930?

A. Paducah.

———◆———

Q. How many fumbles were lost by Western Kentucky's football team while playing against Tampa in 1963?

A. Seven.

———◆———

Q. What was the first pro team to sign Claude Virden following his career at Murray State University?

A. Seattle SuperSonics.

———◆———

Q. In 1967 Western Kentucky University walked away as champions of what basketball tournament in Miami?

A. Hurricane Classic.

Q. Who set a Western Kentucky individual record during the 1980–81 season with twenty-five dunks?

A. Tony Wilson.

———◆———

Q. In what season did Western Kentucky University capture its first OVC basketball championship?

A. 1948–49.

———◆———

Q. The University of Louisville's Browning Nagle set a Fiesta Bowl record with how many yards thrown against Alabama on January 1, 1991?

A. 451.

———◆———

Q. William McCrocklin, who in 1938 became Western Kentucky University's first All-American in basketball, was known by what nickname?

A. Red.

———◆———

Q. What was the amount of the purse at the first running of the Kentucky Derby?

A. $2,850.

———◆———

Q. What swimmer received a Western Kentucky University Athlete-of-the-Year Award for the 1973–74 season?

A. Rick Yeloushan.

———◆———

Q. On what date did Murray State University's Racer Arena open?

A. December 11, 1954.

Q. In what year did Western Kentucky University introduce soccer as a competitive sport in its athletic program?

A. 1982.

Q. In 1941 what horse became the first to win the Kentucky Derby by eight lengths?

A. Whirlaway.

Q. Who served as head football coach at the University of Kentucky from 1969 to 1972?

A. John Ray.

Q. Whom did Muhammad Ali knock out in 1964 to win his first of three heavyweight boxing titles?

A. Sonny Liston.

Q. What years did Darrell Griffith play basketball at the University of Louisville?

A. 1976–80.

Q. Where did Paul Sanderford coach prior to joining Western Kentucky University in 1982 as head women's basketball coach?

A. Louisburg Junior College, North Carolina.

Q. What Louisville facility is the home of the world-famous Kentucky Derby?

A. Churchill Downs.

Q. How many points did Jeff Martin score during his 1986–89 career at Murray State University?

A. 2,484.

———◆———

Q. In a 1969 fans' poll, what Kentuckian was named as all-time Dodgers' shortstop?

A. Pee Wee Reese.

———◆———

Q. What years did Jimmy Feix serve as head football coach at Western Kentucky University?

A. 1968–83.

———◆———

Q. What two-time governor of Kentucky and U.S. senator served as baseball commissioner from 1945 to 1951?

A. Albert Benjamin ("Happy") Chandler.

———◆———

Q. How many total points were scored by the University of Louisville football team during their 1932 season?

A. Eighteen.

———◆———

Q. Who served as Western Kentucky University's first head football coach in 1913?

A. M. A. Leiper.

———◆———

Q. What Murray State University basketball player was the nation's leading rebounder in 1967 with a 21.8 per game average?

A. Dick Cunningham.

Q. Who coached the Lady Toppers' basketball team during the 1925–26 season?

A. Nell Robbins.

◆

Q. The Kentucky Futurity, the state's long-running trotting classic, is held in what city?

A. Lexington.

◆

Q. What nickname was given 1964 ACC Player of the Year and All-American basketball guard Jeff Mullins?

A. Pork Chop.

◆

Q. Greg Campbell set a University of Louisville record with what length punt return playing against Memphis State on November 7, 1970?

A. Ninety-six yards.

◆

Q. At what Fayette County facility is the High Hope Steeplechase held?

A. Kentucky Horse Park.

◆

Q. In 1935 what Western Kentucky University football player received All-KIAC (Kentucky Intercollegiate Athletic Conference) honors?

A. Clarence Caple.

◆

Q. What great shortstop came to the National League to play for Louisville in the last half of the 1897 season?

A. John Peter ("Honus") Wagner.

SCIENCE & NATURE

C H A P T E R S I X

Q. Lee County provides the National Weather Service with winter weather predictions based on what local insect?

A. Woolly worm.

———◆———

Q. At 382 miles, what is the longest river in Kentucky?

A. Green River.

———◆———

Q. In the 1850s, what salad vegetable was developed at Frankfort by John Bibb?

A. Bibb lettuce.

———◆———

Q. Grant's Lick was known for the manufacture of what commodity as early as 1793?

A. Salt.

———◆———

Q. Where did Colonel Harland Sanders develop his fried chicken recipe of eleven secret herbs and spices in the late 1940s?

A. Corbin.

Q. What natural resource was discovered near Hazard in 1917?

A. Oil.

———————◆———————

Q. What type of skins was shipped by the thousands from Louisa to Europe to be fabricated into headware for Napoleon's grenadiers?

A. Bear skins.

———————◆———————

Q. Where is the only documented moonbow in North America?

A. Cumberland Falls.

———————◆———————

Q. What county is known as the "Crappie Capital of the World"?

A. Trigg.

———————◆———————

Q. Constructed in 1896 at a cost of $396,305, what was the first movable needle-type dam to be built in the nation?

A. Big Sandy Dam.

———————◆———————

Q. Who discovered Mammoth Onyx Cave in 1799?
A. Martha Woodson.

———————◆———————

Q. What was the weight of the state record rockfish that Roger Foster caught in Lake Cumberland on December 11, 1985?

A. Fifty-eight pounds, four ounces.

Q. American bison are featured at what wildlife facility near Horse Cave?

A. Kentucky Buffalo Park.

———◆———

Q. Who is credited with having produced the first raw silk in the state at Somerset around 1840?

A. Cyrenius Wait.

———◆———

Q. Who discovered and named Royal Spring in 1774?

A. Col. John Floyd.

———◆———

Q. The Maupin Walker foxhound breed traces its pedigree to the dogs belonging to what Madison County fox hunter of the early 1800s?

A. Gen. George Washington Maupin.

———◆———

Q. At what Rockcastle County site was material mined for use in the manufacture of gunpowder during the Civil War?

A. Great Saltpeter Cave.

———◆———

Q. What facility was built by the State Fish and Game Commission in Whitley County in 1929?

A. Gatliffe Fish Hatchery.

———◆———

Q. Established in 1928, what was the first state park in Kentucky?

A. Pine Mountain State Park.

Q. What Kentucky cave contains one of the nation's largest pre-Columbian Indian burial grounds?

A. Crystal Onyx Cave.

—————◆—————

Q. What was the source of the state's first public water supply, which was begun in Frankfort in 1804?

A. Cedar Cove Spring.

—————◆—————

Q. In 1809 what Danville surgeon performed the nation's first ovariotomy?

A. Dr. Ephraim McDowell.

—————◆—————

Q. The local term "goose nests" describes what geological formation in the Green River cave region?

A. Sinkholes.

—————◆—————

Q. Where was a gunpowder mill erected in Barren County in 1813?

A. Glasgow (on Coon Creek).

—————◆—————

Q. What unusual natural rock shelter of archeological interest is near Cub Run?

A. The Castle.

—————◆—————

Q. The town of Horse Cave is built partially over what cave?

A. Hidden River Cave.

Q. What is the constant temperature in Mammoth Cave?

A. Fifty-four degrees Fahrenheit.

———◆———

Q. As it crosses western Kentucky, U.S. 41 basically follows the ancient migratory route of what indigenous large animal?

A. Bison.

———◆———

Q. Lost River Cave is in what county?
A. Warren.

———◆———

Q. Who was the first person to mine and use coal in Webster County?

A. Alfred Townes.

———◆———

Q. What important byproduct in the production of whiskey is used to feed livestock?

A. Mash, a grain mixture.

———◆———

Q. What record high temperature for Kentucky was recorded at Greensburg on July 28, 1930?

A. 114 degrees Fahrenheit.

———◆———

Q. What type of coal accounts for the majority of Kentucky's production?

A. Bituminous (soft coal).

Q. Kentucky derives its nickname from what prevalent plant in the Lexington area?

A. Bluegrass (the Bluegrass State).

———◆———

Q. What land region comprises the eastern third of the state?

A. Appalachian Plateau.

———◆———

Q. In 1925 what spelunker drew national attention when he became trapped and eventually died while attempting to locate a new entrance to Crystal Cave?

A. Floyd Collins.

———◆———

Q. What noted ornithologist conducted studies across Kentucky from 1808 to 1826?

A. John James Audubon.

———◆———

Q. In which Kentucky county did the first production of ball clay in the United States begin in 1891?

A. Graves.

———◆———

Q. What percentage of Paducah was inundated during the flood of 1937?

A. Ninety percent.

———◆———

Q. The five-mile-long prehistoric canal that connects Bayou De Chien Creek with Obion Creek in the southwestern part of the state is locally known by what name?

A. Lake Slough.

Q. From what Mississippi River community were 50,000 bushels of wheat, 200,000 bushels of corn, and 30,000 dozen turkeys and chickens shipped in 1840?

A. Hickman.

———◆———

Q. What natural disaster in 1811–12 greatly affected the geography of the southwestern tip of the state?

A. The New Madrid earthquake.

———◆———

Q. Whose large fossil collection from Big Bone Lick was later inadvertently ground into fertilizer?

A. Thomas Jefferson.

———◆———

Q. In 1986 what type of raptors successfully nested and hatched two young in Livingston County for the first time since the 1940s?

A. Osprey.

———◆———

Q. How many burley tobacco growers are in Kentucky?
A. 80,000.

———◆———

Q. Where may one of the nation's largest collections of tropical ferns be seen?

A. Kentucky Botanical Gardens (Louisville).

———◆———

Q. How much money was generated in the state by the burley tobacco industry during the fall of 1990?

A. $400,000,000.

Q. The Kentucky Dam, which created one of the nation's largest artificial lakes, was completed in what year?

A. 1944.

---◆---

Q. In 1990 what dollar value was placed on the swine industry in Kentucky?

A. $186,000,000.

---◆---

Q. At its peak productive activity in 1936, how many head of sheep were there in Kentucky?

A. 1.1 million.

---◆---

Q. In 1978 what variety of lespedeza was released by the University of Kentucky?

A. *Appalow sericea.*

---◆---

Q. What name is given to the Kentucky dish of a rich thick soup or broth made from beef, chicken, and vegetables?

A. Burgoo.

---◆---

Q. In the 1850s what Eddyville resident discovered the revolutionary process by which cast and pig iron were converted into steel?

A. William Kelly.

---◆---

Q. What local name was given by early settlers to the unusual six-foot-wide stone bowl shapes cut in the sandstone in Fleming County?

A. Indian kettles.

Q. Approximately how many farms are there in the state?

A. 96,000.

———◆———

Q. What is the highest point in Kentucky, standing 4,145 feet above sea level?

A. Black Mountain.

———◆———

Q. What car manufacturer built a $1.1 billion plant in Scott County in 1985?

A. Toyota.

———◆———

Q. In 1938 what Berea College professor claimed to have discovered ten humanoid footprints imprinted in 250-million-year-old sandstone in Rockcastle County?

A. Dr. Wilbur Burroughs.

———◆———

Q. What is the altitude of Pine Mountain?

A. 2,600 feet above sea level.

———◆———

Q. In 1929 what Kentucky county received a national award for its leadership in the development of purebred Jersey cattle?

A. Calloway.

———◆———

Q. What facility near Owingsville cast cannonballs during the War of 1812?

A. Slate Creek Iron Furnace.

Q. Jeptha Knob in Shelby County is what type of geological formation?

A. Cryptovolcano.

———◆———

Q. What is the height of the Carter Cave Natural Bridge?

A. 196 feet.

———◆———

Q. In which county were Kentucky's first natural gas reserves tapped in 1858?

A. Meade.

———◆———

Q. What six-member state agency was established in 1878 to help deal with epidemics and catastrophes?

A. Board of Health.

———◆———

Q. In Hancock County what forty-acre flat-topped, hand-shaped geological formation rises from the lowlands near the Ohio River?

A. Jeffery Cliff.

———◆———

Q. What Crittenden County mineral has been mined extensively for use in the production of steel?

A. Fluorite (fluorspar).

———◆———

Q. In 1815 a company headed by Andrew Jackson started a mining operation in Kentucky, hoping to extract what precious metal from existing galena deposits?

A. Silver.

Q. What endangered species is found only in Mammoth Cave Park?

A. Kentucky Cave Shrimp.

———◆———

Q. Herrington Lake was formed in 1925 when a dam was completed across what river?

A. Dix River.

———◆———

Q. What is the state's third largest revenue producer and its second largest private employer?

A. Tourism.

———◆———

Q. How many eggs does the female Kentucky cardinal normally lay at a time?

A. Three to five.

———◆———

Q. What marsupial is found in Kentucky?

A. Virginia opossum.

———◆———

Q. What event held at Pleasant Hill each spring features sheep shearing along with the carding, spinning, weaving, and dyeing of wool?

A. Sheep to Shawl.

———◆———

Q. What is the state tree of Kentucky?

A. Kentucky coffeetree.

Q. Where is the "World's Largest Single Stalactite"?

A. Diamond Caverns

------◆------

Q. How many varieties of fish are there in Kentucky?

A. More than 200.

------◆------

Q. Where does Kentucky rank in comparison with the rest of the nation in the production of whiskey?

A. First.

------◆------

Q. What is the clearance of the vast stone arch at Natural Bridge State Resort Park?

A. Ninety-two feet.

------◆------

Q. Where at Berea may a world-wide collection of pre-historic artifacts, fossils, and minerals be seen?

A. Berea College Geology Museum.

------◆------

Q. What is the only variety of hummingbird found in Kentucky?

A. Ruby-throated.

------◆------

Q. Dropping 113 feet, what is Kentucky's highest waterfall?

A. Yahoo Falls.

Q. What commercial cave is at the historic Wondering Woods Village?

A. Majestic Caverns.

———◆———

Q. Consisting of 3,600 acres, what is the largest resort park in the state park system?

A. Lake Barkley State Resort Park.

———◆———

Q. What is Kentucky's most valuable farm product?

A. Tobacco.

———◆———

Q. Which county is the state's leading corn producer?

A. Union.

———◆———

Q. Around 1892 what Murray inventor made the first radio broadcast?

A. Nathan B. Stubblefield.

———◆———

Q. An exhibit showing the world through an insect's eye can be seen at what Louisville attraction?

A. The MetaZoo Education Center at the Louisville Zoological Garden.

———◆———

Q. Each spring what evergreen is honored with a festival at Pine Mountain State Resort Park?

A. Mountain laurel.

Q. What is the average size of a Kentucky farm?

A. 150 acres.

———◆———

Q. Land Between the Lakes is situated between what two large bodies of water?

A. Kentucky Lake and Lake Barkley.

———◆———

Q. In total tobacco products where does Kentucky rank nationally?

A. Second only to North Carolina.

———◆———

Q. What is the state fish?

A. Kentucky bass.

———◆———

Q. Registered with the American Forestry Association, the nation's largest sassafras tree is in what city?

A. Owensboro.

———◆———

Q. Carr Fork Lake is in the southern portion of what county?

A. Knott.

———◆———

Q. What is the nickname of the 4,600-acre Breaks Interstate Park?

A. Grand Canyon of the South.

Q. The seeds of what tree were roasted and used by pioneers as a substitute for coffee beans?

A. Kentucky coffeetree.

———◆———

Q. What three counties account for most of Kentucky's peach production?

A. Henderson, McCracken, and Trimble.

———◆———

Q. What forty-seven-acre facility in Ashland contains prehistoric Indian mounds?

A. Central Park.

———◆———

Q. Which Kentucky cave is noted for its rare crystal onyx rimstone formations?

A. Crystal Onyx Cave.

———◆———

Q. What Pike County lake is known for its largemouth bass, bluegill, and crappie?

A. Fishtrap Lake.

———◆———

Q. During the 1880s at what site in Jackson County were humanoidlike footprints discovered in a layer of carboniferous sandstone?

A. Big Hill.

———◆———

Q. What two rivers flow through Mammoth Cave National Park?

A. Green and Nolin.

Q. The Land Between the Lakes outdoor recreation area covers how many acres?

A. Over 170,000.

———◆———

Q. At what Paducah museum is the nation's second largest shell collection?

A. William Clark Market House Museum.

———◆———

Q. Situated southeast of Elkhorn City, what is the depth of the five-mile-long, 250-million-year-old gorge at Breaks Interstate Park?

A. 1,600 feet.

———◆———

Q. What is Kentucky's second most valuable mined material?

A. Stone.

———◆———

Q. In 1926 what plant was designated by the General Assembly as the official state flower?

A. Goldenrod.

———◆———

Q. How many acres comprise Daniel Boone National Forest?

A. 664,000.

———◆———

Q. At 65 feet in height and 125 feet in width, what is the second largest waterfall east of the Rockies?

A. Cumberland Falls.

Q. With what two other states does Kentucky share the Cumberland Gap National Historical Park?

A. Tennessee and Virginia.

———◆———

Q. What is the elevation of Guntown Mountain?

A. 1,350 feet above sea level.

———◆———

Q. Longbows, crossbows, and flintlock and percussion cap rifles are the only weapons allowed at what hunting area?

A. Pioneer Weapons Hunting Area, Morehead.

———◆———

Q. What is the fourth oldest commercial cave in the United States?

A. Diamond Caverns.

———◆———

Q. Covering 5,600 acres, Laurel River Lake is situated in what national forest?

A. Daniel Boone National Forest.

———◆———

Q. For what grain crop is Calloway County famous?

A. Popcorn.

———◆———

Q. Whose extensive butterfly collection may be viewed at Kentucky State University?

A. King Farouk of Egypt.

Q. What is the official state wild animal?

A. Gray squirrel.

———◆———

Q. The handsome wood of the Kentucky coffeetree is known by what nickname?

A. Kentucky mahogany.

———◆———

Q. Approximately what percentage of the world's bourbon whiskey is produced in Kentucky?

A. 80 percent.

———◆———

Q. Measuring 8,422 feet long and 206 feet high, what is the largest dam in the TVA system?

A. Kentucky Dam.

———◆———

Q. Where may a floral clock featuring a 530-pound minute hand and a 420-pound hour hand be seen?

A. Frankfort.

———◆———

Q. What is the largest spring in Kentucky?

A. Royal Spring.

———◆———

Q. The home and apothecary shop of the nineteenth-century pioneer surgeon, Dr. Ephraim McDowell of Danville, is maintained by what organization?

A. Kentucky Medical Association.

Q. Central Kentucky's Bluegrass region is known by what nickname?

A. Horse Capital of the World.

———◆———

Q. What surgeon, who pioneered transplant surgery featuring the Jarvik-7 mechanical heart, relocated to Louisville in 1984?

A. William C. DeVries.

———◆———

Q. For his work in what area did Kentuckian Thomas Hunt Morgan receive a Nobel Prize?

A. Genetics.

———◆———

Q. How many bourbon distilleries are there in Kentucky?

A. Sixteen.

———◆———

Q. In what park is a one-half-mile-long, by one-third-mile-wide pyramid of rocks?

A. Breaks Interstate Park.

———◆———

Q. Nolin Lake is situated in what three counties?

A. Edmonson, Grayson, and Hart.

———◆———

Q. In what year was Mammoth Cave National Park established by the federal government?

A. 1941.

Q. At what Fort Campbell facility is the only World War II cargo glider on display in the United States?

A. Don F. Pratt Museum.

———◆———

Q. What is the length of the locks at Barkley Dam?

A. 1,200 feet.

———◆———

Q. How many miles of scenic woodland trails are there in the Land Between the Lakes?

A. 200.

———◆———

Q. Occupied from 800 to 1350 A.D., what Indian ceremonial site and trade center is near the confluence of the Ohio and Mississippi rivers?

A. Wickliffe Mounds.

———◆———

Q. What Kentucky river is designated as a national river and recreation area?

A. Big South Fork River.

———◆———

Q. During the War of 1812, what mineral was mined in Mammoth Cave for the manufacture of gunpowder?

A. Saltpeter.

———◆———

Q. What promontory gives a scenic view of Hazard and the north fork of the Kentucky River?

A. Peter's Peak.

Q. The Wolf Creek Dam creates what 101-mile-long lake?

A. Lake Cumberland.

———◆———

Q. What Land Between the Lakes' facility allows visitors to see the workings of a contemporary farm with domesticated animals?

A. Empire Farm.

———◆———

Q. The National Audubon Society operates what 275-acre sanctuary in Kentucky?

A. Buckley Wildlife Sanctuary.

———◆———

Q. Where may the country's oldest moonshine still be seen?

A. American Outpost, Clermont.

———◆———

Q. How many tons of coal were used to construct the Coal House at Middlesboro in 1926?

A. Forty.

———◆———

Q. Featuring over 500 pieces of communications equipment, the Pioneer Telephone Museum is in what city?

A. Winchester.

———◆———

Q. Situated in the Land Between the Lakes, what facility presents films and interpretive displays of native plants and animals?

A. Woodlands Nature Center.

Q. Where in Louisville may machines producing 5,000 cigarettes an hour be seen?

A. Philip Morris USA.

———◆———

Q. Varying in width from twenty to sixty feet, what is the largest river in Mammoth Cave?

A. Echo.

———◆———

Q. The treeless area in the southern mid-section of the state was given what name by the early pioneers?

A. The Barrens.

———◆———

Q. What scenic Kentucky lake is situated at the northwestern tip of Logan County?

A. Lake Malone.

———◆———

Q. The Kentucky River palisades are preserved in what 274-acre nature area?

A. Raven Run Nature Sanctuary.

———◆———

Q. What is the incubation period of the Kentucky cardinal?

A. Twelve to thirteen days.

———◆———

Q. Featuring exhibits and a multimedia presentation, what facility at the Kentucky Horse Park is dedicated to Kentucky's only native breed of horse?

A. American Saddle Horse Museum.

Q. Where does Kentucky rank nationally in the production of burley tobacco?

A. First.

———◆———

Q. At what University of Kentucky facility may exhibits of the cultural history of Kentucky and the development of man be seen?

A. Anthropology Museum.

———◆———

Q. What 10,050-acre lake is situated in Barren and Allen counties?

A. Barren River Lake.

———◆———

Q. Red River Gorge is in what state park?

A. Natural Bridge State Resort Park.

———◆———

Q. What Kentucky fishing spot is considered the best in the nation for catching muskies?

A. Cave Run.

———◆———

Q. Coal mining exhibits are featured at what Greenville facility?

A. Duncan Cultural Center.

———◆———

Q. Who founded the Frontier Nursing Service, recognized as the nation's oldest school of nurse-midwifery, at Hayden in 1925?

A. Mary Breckinridge.

Q. What state park is situated seven miles northeast of Olive Hill?

A. Carter Caves State Resort Park.

———◆———

Q. What natural passage served as a gateway through the Appalachians for settlers moving westward into Kentucky and Tennessee?

A. Cumberland Gap.

———◆———

Q. At what Levi Jackson Wilderness Road State Park attraction is one of the world's largest collections of millstones?

A. McHargue's Mill.

———◆———

Q. What two types of vultures are found in Kentucky?

A. Black and turkey.

———◆———

Q. Jesse James Cave is near what community?

A. Park City.

———◆———

Q. What site in Pike County represents one of the nation's largest engineering and earth-moving achievements?

A. The Pikeville Cut-Thru.

———◆———

Q. Situated in the eastern part of the state, what is the span of the Sky Bridge formation?

A. Ninety feet.